Blender Baby Food

Over 125 Recipes
for Healthy Homemade Meals

Nicole Young
Nadine Day, RD, Nutritional Adviser

Robert
ROSE

For complete cataloguing information, see page 182.

Disclaimer
The recipes in this book have been carefully tested by our kitchen and our tasters. To the best of our knowledge, they are safe and nutritious for ordinary use and users. For those people with food or other allergies, or who have special food requirements or health issues, please read the suggested contents of each recipe carefully and determine whether or not they may create a problem for you. All recipes are used at the risk of the consumer.

We cannot be responsible for any hazards, loss or damage that may occur as a result of any recipe use.

For those with special needs, allergies, requirements or health problems, in the event of any doubt, please contact your medical adviser prior to the use of any recipe.

Design & Production: PageWave Graphics Inc.
Editor: Sue Sumeraj
Food Tester: Jennifer MacKenzie
Proofreader: Sheila Wawanash
Index: Belle Wong
Cover Photo: © A. B./Corbis

We acknowledge the financial support of the Government of Canada through the Book Publishing Industry Development Program (BPIDP) for our publishing activities.

Published by Robert Rose Inc.
120 Eglinton Avenue East, Suite 800, Toronto, Ontario, Canada M4P 1E2
Tel: (416) 322-6552; Fax: (416) 322-6936

Printed in Canada
4 5 6 7 8 9 CPL 13 12 11 10 09 08 07

Contents

Preface

A month before I gave birth to my first child, I attended a birthday party for a friend's son. I observed the "veteran" parents escorting their toddlers to the table at mealtime and stared in utter amazement at my friend's son, who sat proudly in his high chair and proceeded to eat his first birthday meal of blanched broccoli and green beans, strips of red peppers and carrots, while the neighboring children pushed away everything but fish crackers. What had my friend done to produce this veggie- and hummus-loving pita eater? As I watched him eat his body weight in produce, I heard his mother's words: "I made all his food from scratch." I was sold.

Over the past five years, I have taught hundreds of classes to parents and caregivers about the merits of preparing their own food for babies. We discuss the issues of variety, quality, ability to graduate textures and cost effectiveness. I demonstrate the simplicity of preparing a variety of purées, even for sleep-deprived parents whose last wish is have an extra task added to their baby-dominated lives. All of these details are included in Nadine's comprehensive introduction.

While it has been many years since I had to make my own purées, the benefits are undeniable. I have two healthy eaters, who still enjoy treats but don't turn their noses up at a platter of fresh veggies. I am fortunate.

More than anything, I want this book to inspire you to give making your own baby food a try. May you and your child have many happy memories of the food from these pages…

Acknowledgments

I have to thank Liam and Claire for being my inspiration to make baby food and David for giving me our inspirations and providing the time, support and encouragement to finish this book. I love you all more than food! It was the ideal year for taste testers, as we had eleven babies born to friends, and I am very appreciative of all the discerning palates. May you all be healthy eaters with massive appetites!

Thanks to Andrew Chase for recommending me, publisher Bob Dees for giving me the project, and my lawyer, sister and friend Danielle for looking out for me since we were little. Thanks also to my sister Stephanie for her blender wisdom. I'd like to express my gratitude to Nadine Day, registered dietitian extraordinaire, for her advice and nutritional analysis, and to Judy Coveney for introducing us. Thanks to Sue Sumeraj, our patient editor, for teaching me the process and making me seem literate.

Finally, eternal thanks to my mom and dad for showing me what it means to be a great parent and teaching me that anything is possible.

— Nicole Young

I would like to thank my daughter, Grace, for teaching me more about infant feeding than any course I have ever taken. Thanks also to my husband, Simon, and my mom for all their support and for making sure I have a quiet space in which to write. And to my dad, whose voice always echoes that I can do whatever I set my mind to. I love you all so much.

I am in debt to Nicole Young and Judy Coveney for encouraging me to take on this project. Convincing me was a challenge, because they contacted me on my first day of being a new mom.

Special thanks to my friends and colleagues Liane Evans and Karem Kalin for critiquing the facts and to our editor, Sue Sumeraj, for making my words sound great.

This has been a very valuable and rewarding experience, and I am so happy I took advantage of the opportunity.

— Nadine Day

Introduction

It is exciting when your baby starts to eat solid food. He is making an important step towards toddlerhood! Helping a child progress through this stage can be very rewarding. Parents often have many questions about when to start solids and what to feed when. The good news is that it is not an exact science. There are a few suggested guidelines, but the real judge is your baby. He will give you cues that he is ready to move on to a new flavor or texture.

Making your own baby food may seem challenging at first, but it doesn't have to be. *Blender Baby Food* provides many recipes and tips that will make baby food fun and exciting for you and your baby. Whether you choose to make all of your own baby food or just some of it, the blender is a great way to offer new flavors in a baby-friendly texture. Even when your child is eating table food, there is always room for a fruit smoothie or a nutritious dip.

When to Start Solids

The American Academy of Pediatrics and Health Canada recommend starting complementary foods at six months. Complementary foods means foods *in addition* to breast milk or formula. At this point, babies are both mentally and physiologically ready to accept solid foods. But every baby is different when it comes to readiness to start solid foods. Your baby may be ready if she:

- can sit alone or with minimal support;
- opens her mouth when she sees something coming towards her face or mouth;
- turns her head away when she does not want it;
- closes her lips over the spoon; and
- seems interested in what you are eating.

Follow your baby's lead. It may take one or two months before she is eating a few tablespoons of solid food at one time. Infants can thrive on breast milk or formula alone until six months, so there is no need to rush into solid foods.

What Foods to Start When

Children progress at very different rates. Let your child help you assess when he is ready to start making the move from exclusively breast or bottle feedings to table foods.

At **six months** of age, iron stores your baby acquired from you during pregnancy start to decline, and an additional source of iron is required. Iron-fortified infant cereal is usually the first food introduced to infants. It is best to start with single-grain cereals, such as rice or barley, introduced one at a time to help your child's body adapt to the new food and so you can watch for symptoms of an allergic reaction. Then you can phase in oatmeal and finally mixed-grain cereals containing wheat.

Once your child is eating 2 to 3 tablespoons (25 to 45 mL) of single-grain cereal a couple of times a day, you can start to introduce vegetables and fruits. It does not matter whether you start with vegetables or with fruits. Some people find that their children eat more vegetables if they were offered before fruit. Some don't find any difference. Let your child take the lead, but don't give up if he rejects a food on the first attempt. He might just be surprised by the new flavor.

It will be much easier for you to identify potential allergies or intolerances if you introduce new foods five to seven days apart. This is especially important if you have a family history of food allergies.

Continue breastfeeding or formula feeding on demand while you are introducing infant cereals, vegetables and fruits. Breast milk or formula is your child's best source of protein, fat and many vitamins and minerals, such as calcium. At this point, solid foods should be *in addition* to your regular breast milk or formula feedings.

At **seven or eight months**, your child will probably be eating a variety of vegetables and fruits, as well as iron-fortified infant cereals, two to three times a day. He can now begin to try other grain products, such as strips of bread, toast, crackers and wheat cereals. Make sure these foods are cut or broken into bite-size pieces.

At this age, your baby will also be ready to try meat, poultry, fish and meat-alternative products such as egg yolks and puréed cooked dried beans and lentils. (Egg whites have been shown to cause an allergic reaction in some children; therefore, it is recommended that you wait until your child is at least one year old before you introduce them.)

Some children initially have difficulty accepting meat products. Make sure they are puréed or finely minced with a little water or broth, or with a vegetable. There are many creative meat and vegetable combinations in this book. Puréed foods should have the consistency of smooth pudding, while the texture of minced food will be similar to rice pudding. The longer you run your blender, the smoother the consistency will be. To be on the safe side, introduce new foods five to seven days apart. Let your baby get comfortable with a new flavor before you introduce the next one.

At this age, babies are ready to try using a cup. Breast milk, formula and water are good choices to offer in a regular cup or a "sippy" cup. Juice is not necessary, especially if your child is eating vegetables and fruits. It is good practice for children to learn to eat rather than drink their fruit. Whole fruits have the added benefit of fiber, which is important to good health. When given the choice, many toddlers will drink their calories, and the juice cup can sometimes be abused. Juice is also high in sugar and may lead to increased dental cavities. If you serve juice, make sure it is 100% fruit juice diluted with water, and serve no more than 4 ounces (125 mL) per day.

At **nine to twelve months**, your child can start to eat dairy foods such as yogurt and cheese. At this time, he can usually eat adapted table food: diced cooked vegetables and fruits, tender chopped meats and casseroles with noodles cut up.

It is important to introduce your child to a variety of textures, as this helps him learn to chew and swallow properly and safely. The following chart gives an idea of what textures are appropriate at what age:

TIP: Use the large side of a grater to cut up harder fruits and vegetables such as carrots, apples and pears. Finely dice softer cooked foods into $1/2$-inch (1 cm) cubes (the size of the tip of your pinky finger).

6 months	Very watery purées, the consistency of watered-down pudding
7 months	Slightly lumpy minced foods, the consistency of rice or tapioca pudding
8 to 12 months	Soft foods, diced or shredded
12 months and over	Adapted family foods (soft foods or harder foods diced into bite-size pieces)

At this age, your child's main beverage is still breast milk or formula. Whole pasteurized cow's milk can be started after one year and can replace formula or be given in addition to breast milk. It is not appropriate for children to be on a fat-restricted diet; they need the extra energy and essential fatty acids that homogenized milk provides for proper growth and development. At two years, toddlers can be switched to 2% or 1% milk.

Age Appropriateness

The recipes in this book are broken into chapters according to the age at which foods generally become appropriate and tolerable to most babies. Here's a general idea of what foods are appropriate when:

6 months	Single vegetables and fruits (after single-grain cereal has been introduced); mixed vegetables and fruits (after all ingredients in the recipe have been introduced separately)
7 months	Pasta, rice, other grains
8 months	Meat, poultry, fish, lentils, egg yolks
9 months	Yogurt, cheese
12 months	Homogenized milk, honey, egg whites. Talk to your doctor about adding nuts and nut butters.

Remember, these are just suggestions. Your pediatrician or family doctor may suggest otherwise, especially if your family has a history of allergies or intolerances.

Again, when it comes to textures and flavors, let your baby guide you: she will let you know when she is ready for something new.

Meal Plans

At the beginning of each chapter, you will find three meal plans to help you get started. Each recipe makes about 4 to 8 servings. To save time and freezer space, use the same meal plan four days in a row, then move on to a new meal plan. Infants and toddlers do not crave variety the way adults do.

Remember, children are all different sizes and have different needs. Infants and toddlers have erratic eating patterns and may eat more one day and less the next. Over time it will equal out.

Safety Concerns

Honey

Health Canada recommends that honey not be fed to children who are less than one year old. Honey is a risk factor for infant botulism. Botulism is life-threatening food poisoning caused by the presence of the botulinus toxin produced by the *Clostridium botulinum* bacterium. The amount of botulism present in honey should not be harmful to adults, but it is harmful to infants. Make sure to read packages and recipes carefully, as honey is often used to sweeten foods.

TIP: *For recipes with a combination of ingredients, it is best to first introduce each food separately so you can watch for any food reactions.*

Eggs

Eggshells occasionally become contaminated with salmonella bacteria. Cook all eggs very well and avoid all foods containing raw eggs.

Choking

Here are some guidelines to help you avoid this hazard:

- Supervise your infant at all times while he is eating.
- Make sure mealtimes are quiet and calm.
- Don't make your child laugh while he is eating: it could cause him to inhale food.
- Avoid hard, small, round and sticky foods, which can block the airway (see the examples in the chart below for making such foods safe).
- Don't give the following foods to children under four: popcorn, hard candies, gum, cough drops, raisins, peanuts or other nuts, sunflower seeds, fish with bones, or foods with toothpicks or skewers.

Preparing Foods Safely

Food	Unsafe preparation	Safer preparation
Hot dogs/wieners	Sliced into rounds	Cut lengthwise and then into half-moons
Raw carrots or hard fresh fruits	Whole or large pieces	Grated
Fruits with pits	Whole	Diced with pits removed
Grapes	Whole	Chopped
Peanut butter	Spoonful or alone	Spread thinly on crackers or bread

Bottles

Babies should be supervised while using a bottle. The safest way to feed a bottle is when your child is sitting upright in a quiet setting where he is not distracted from eating. The bottle should not be given "propped up" by a blanket or towel or when your child is lying down, walking, running or in a car.

Food Allergies

Food allergies occur when the body has an adverse response to an ingested food. The symptoms may include anaphylaxis (a life-threatening reaction), stomach pain, diarrhea, rash around the mouth or anus, nausea, vomiting, stomach cramps, itching (throat, mouth, eyes), hives, swelling, stuffy nose, runny nose, shortness of breath and difficulty swallowing. The severity of the reaction depends on the severity of the allergy. If you suspect that your child is having an adverse reaction, see your doctor.

The development of a food allergy is mostly genetic: if a child's mother, father or sibling is allergic to a food, she has an increased chance of also being allergic to that food. But food allergies can also develop when a potentially allergenic food is introduced to an infant too early. The chance of developing an allergy is higher in the first year of life because the infant's intestinal system is more permeable to (allows in) food allergens. Milk, eggs, peanuts, soy, nuts and wheat are responsible for 95% of all food allergies. Studies indicate that 2% to 8% of infants and children under three will experience food hypersensitivity. However, many children outgrow their allergies by their fifth birthday. If your family has a history of food allergies, or if you have any concerns, talk to your doctor before introducing any potentially allergenic food.

If your child is diagnosed with a food allergy or intolerance, talk to your doctor or dietitian about any nutritional deficiencies that may result. For example, if your child is allergic to or cannot tolerate milk, she may have to take a calcium supplement or increase her consumption of other calcium-rich foods to meet her needs.

Making Your Own Baby Food

Baby food doesn't have to come in jars. Making your own at home is not difficult. Baby food is simply strained, puréed or mashed adult food, just a different version of the food you prepare for yourself. Here are three good reasons to make your own baby food:

- You know what's in it.
- You can tailor the texture to your baby's preferences.
- You can shape your baby's tastes and help him learn what fresh foods taste like.

Tips for Making Baby Food

- Work under the most sanitary conditions possible:
  - ✳ Scrub your hands with hot water and soap, rinse and dry with a clean towel before fixing your baby's food, before feeding your baby and after changing your baby's diapers.
  - ✳ Scrub all working surfaces with soap and hot water.
  - ✳ Scrub all equipment with soap and hot water, and rinse well.
- Prepare fresh fruits and vegetables by scrubbing, paring or peeling and removing seeds.
- Prepare meats by removing all bones, skin, connective tissue, gristle and fat.
- Cook foods, when necessary, by boiling them until tender in a small covered saucepan with a small amount of water. The amount of water is important: the less water used, the more nutrients stay in the food.
- Purée food using a blender, food processor, baby food grinder, spoon or fork. Grind up tough foods. Cut food into small pieces or thin slices. Remove seeds and pits from fruit.

- There's no need to add salt or sugar. Try a bit of lemon juice as both a preservative and a natural flavor enhancer.
- Avoid deep-frying, which adds unhealthy fats to foods.
- Don't feel you have to prepare separate meals for your baby. You can simply take portions of your adult food (before you add strong seasonings) and grind or mash it to a consistency appropriate for your baby.
- Make enough purée for several meals and store as directed below or in the recipe.

To Store

- If you're not using puréed food right away, refrigerate or freeze it in portioned containers. Most refrigerated foods will last up to three days (exceptions are noted in the recipes).
- To freeze: Pour cooled, puréed food into paper cupcake liners or a clean ice cube tray and cover with plastic wrap or foil. When frozen solid (after about twenty-four hours), transfer cubes to a resealable freezer bag labeled with the contents and date.
- Rotate stock as the supermarket does, putting the most recently frozen foods behind the previously frozen ones. Homemade baby foods can be safely kept frozen for three months.

To Thaw/Reheat

- For slow thawing, place a day's worth of baby food in a sealed container in the refrigerator. It will thaw in about four hours. Do not thaw at room temperature, as bacteria could grow in the food while it is thawing.
- For fast thawing and heating, heat frozen cubes in a heat-resistant container in a pan of hot water over low heat or in the microwave.
- Stir the food well and test it with a finger to be sure it's not too hot (especially if you use a microwave). Babies generally like their food close to room temperature.
- Discard any food that has been heated and not eaten.

Equipment Needed

- **Blender:** All of the recipes in this book work best using the blender.
- **Fine-mesh sieve or strainer:** Use for juices, soft fruits and vegetables (but not meats). Press food through the sieve with the back of a spoon — to remove seeds, for example.
- **Spoons, forks and a potato masher:** Use to mash soft foods — most canned fruits, egg yolks, bananas and potatoes — to the right consistency.
- **Food mill:** The smaller-size baby food mill is similar to the larger version and can be purchased in the baby section of department stores. It can be used at home or when traveling. It is great for puréeing soft vegetables, fruits, pasta and rice.
- **Plastic ice cube trays:** Use to freeze extra food as explained opposite.

Additional Useful Equipment

- Food processor
- Hand-held blender
- Vegetable brush and peeler
- Saucepan with lid
- Vegetable steamer
- Egg poacher
- Roasting pan
- Cookie sheet
- Muffin tin
- Ovenproof glass cups
- Measuring cups and spoons
- Ladle
- Spatula
- Sharp paring knife
- Cutting board
- Grater
- Storage jars (4 oz/125 mL)
- Small freezer bags
- Waxed paper
- Freezer tape
- Marking pen

Twelve to Twenty-four Months: Learning Healthy Eating

At one year old, your baby officially becomes a toddler. She is on the move, and it may seem like she has no desire to eat regular meals and snacks. This is normal. Try to give your toddler frequent small feedings rather than the traditional meals and snacks. Providing toddlers with healthy food choices gives them the energy and nutrients they need to grow and helps them develop a taste for a wide variety of foods. You will have more success if you feed your toddler nutritious foods when she is hungry than you will if you force her to sit and eat at certain times. This does not mean that toddlers should not be a part of family meals. Your toddler learns a lot from sitting at the family table and seeing how the rest of the family enjoys healthy meals together.

After their first year, children's growth rates slow down. That is why toddlers' eating habits may seem minimal, erratic and unpredictable. During the first year of life, children typically triple their birth weight, and their length increases by 50%. However, their weight will not quadruple until age two, and their length will not double again until age four. They simply do not need the volume of food they did in the first year. Letting your child tell you when she is hungry allows her to follow her own instincts when it comes to regulating food intake. Your job as a parent is to make sure your child has a variety of healthy foods available when she is hungry.

A good way to learn about healthy eating is to look at the American Food Pyramid or Canada's Food Guide to Healthy Eating. The serving sizes in these guides are designed for people over four years of age, but they are a great starting point when you're deciding what foods to offer your child. Both guides focus on the four major food groups: grain products, vegetables and fruits, milk products and meat and alternatives. Each food group provides unique nutrients, so it is important to offer your child a variety of foods from each food group every day. A good rule of thumb is to aim for three of the four food groups at each meal and one or two of the food groups at each snack. This will ensure that your child gets all the nutrients she needs to grow and develop.

You can download a copy of the American Food Pyramid at **www.nal.usda.gov/fnic/Fpyr/pyramid.html**. You can download a copy of Canada's Food Guide to Healthy Eating at www.hc-sc.gc.ca/hpfb-dgpsa/onpp-bppn/food_guide_rainbow_e.html, or you can request one from your local public health office.

The Dietary Reference Intake (DRI) is the recommended daily intake of certain key nutrients, such as carbohydrates, protein, fat, calcium, vitamin C, fiber, iron and many more. These have been developed, in a joint effort by American and Canadian nutrition experts, to expand and replace the former American Recommended Dietary Allowance (RDA) and Canadian Recommended Nutrient Intake (RNI). Adequate Intake (AI) is the recommended average daily intake level. Aim to give your child this amount. The Tolerable Upper Limit (UI) is the highest average daily nutrient intake level that is likely to pose no risk of adverse health effects to almost all individuals in the general population.

Grain Products

Grain products provide most of the energy your toddler needs throughout the day. Grain products can also be a great source of fiber, vitamins and minerals, especially iron. Always choose whole grains or enriched products. Healthy examples are whole-grain or 100% whole wheat bread, high-fiber cereal and whole wheat or enriched pasta.

TIP: *The term "enriched" means that a food such as white flour or white pasta has some of the vitamins added back into it after processing.*

Nutrient Highlight: Fiber

Fiber is an essential part of a healthy diet for everyone, including infants and toddlers. Fiber is found in the cell walls of plants and is made up of a number of complex carbohydrates that cannot be digested by the body.

Fiber is essential for healthy bowel function, and a diet rich in fiber has many health benefits. We need to eat fiber foods such as grain products every day to maintain the health of our digestive systems and prevent heart disease.

Dietary Reference Intake for Fiber

0 to 6 months	Not determined
7 to 12 months	Not determined
1 to 3 years	19 g/day (AI)

There are two main types of fiber: soluble and insoluble. **Soluble fiber** is soluble in water and absorbs water like a sponge, swelling and therefore increasing the bulk of the intestines' contents. Soluble fiber can be found in such foods as apples, pears, oats, barley, psyllium, prunes and beans. Research shows that soluble fiber plays a significant role in lowering blood cholesterol levels, thereby reducing the risk of coronary heart disease. **Insoluble fiber** is not soluble in water and has the ability to speed up the rate at which food moves along the intestines. Therefore, an increase in insoluble fiber intake is recommended to help alleviate constipation. Wheat, wheat bran and seeds are excellent sources of insoluble fiber.

When choosing grain products, look for breads that have 2 grams or more fiber per slice and cereals that have more than 4 grams of fiber per serving. Good sources of fiber include whole grains, wheat bran, beans, lentils and most fruits and vegetables.

Vegetables and Fruits

TIP: Don't forget frozen vegetables and fruits — they are usually packed when the products are at their peak and can be more economical when fresh produce is not in season. Canned vegetables are not recommended for infants due to their high sodium content. If you must use canned products, rinse them thoroughly to reduce the sodium.

Vegetables and fruits provide carbohydrate, fiber, vitamins (especially A and C) and minerals. This food group is often the most difficult for parents. Try making it fun! Use playful words such as "carrot coins" and "broccoli trees." Many of the recipes in this book combine vegetables and fruits with other food groups, which may make them more acceptable to your toddler. Most importantly, your toddler should watch you enjoying vegetables and fruits. It is not fair to expect your child to eat something you won't eat!

Dark leafy green and bright orange or red vegetables and fruits pack the most nutrients. Broccoli, spinach, squash, sweet potatoes, carrots, cantaloupe, bell peppers and berries are all great choices. Make sure that your child eats a variety of fruits and vegetables, since each offers a different combination of the vitamins and minerals essential to good health

Nutrient Highlight: Vitamin C

The body needs vitamin C to help with healing and the development of connective tissue and healthy gums. It has been said to reduce the symptoms and duration of the common cold. Vitamin C also plays an important role in helping the body absorb iron.

Dietary Reference Intake for Vitamin C

0 to 6 months	40 mg/day (AI)
7 to 12 months	50 mg/day (AI)
1 to 3 years	15 mg/day (AI); 400 mg/day (UI)

Good sources of vitamin C include citrus fruits, tomatoes, potatoes, Brussels sprouts, cauliflower, broccoli, strawberries, cabbage, spinach and bell peppers.

Milk Products

Milk products are your child's main source of calcium and vitamin D, which are essential for strong bones and teeth. This group also provides protein, fat, vitamins and minerals. Children between twelve and twenty-four months of age require more fat and should therefore drink whole or homogenized milk. Lower-fat 2% or 1% milk can be introduced after two years. Other healthy choices include cheese and whole-milk yogurt.

Nutrient Highlight: Calcium and Vitamin D

Calcium doesn't just help build strong bones and teeth; it is also needed for muscles such as the heart to contract, blood to clot and nerve impulses to transmit. Your bones act as a storehouse for calcium. If your calcium needs are not met through the foods you eat, it will be withdrawn from your bones.

Milk products are excellent sources of calcium. However, only fluid milk and some yogurts contain vitamin D, which helps our body absorb calcium and is equally important for bone health.

Dietary Reference Intake for Calcium

0 to 6 months	210 mg/day (AI)
7 to 12 months	270 mg/day (AI)
1 to 3 years	500 mg/day (AI)

Good sources of calcium include milk, yogurt and cheese. Good sources of vitamin D include fluid milk, egg yolks, high-fat fish and sunshine.

Meat and Alternatives

The meat and alternatives group provides a great source of protein and iron, as well as fat, vitamins and minerals. Make sure that meat is cut up into bite-size pieces, as it is sometimes hard for little teeth to chew. Healthy choices include lean beef, lamb, pork, chicken without skin and fish, especially fatty fish such as salmon.

Don't forget the alternatives! Eggs, peanut butter, tofu, beans and legumes are great sources of protein and add variety to your toddler's diet. Beans and legumes are also great sources of fiber.

Nutrient Highlight: Iron

Iron is a component of blood that helps carry oxygen. Iron deficiency is common in North America, and people who do not get enough iron can develop iron deficiency anemia. The symptoms include tiredness, irritability and loss of the ability to concentrate. Anemia can cause behavior and developmental problems in children. Iron from animal sources is called **heme iron** and is better absorbed by the body. Iron from non-animal sources is called **non-heme iron** and can be better absorbed if eaten with a food high in vitamin C.

The iron requirements of infants and children are very high. In the first six months, these iron needs are met by the stores they received from their mother during pregnancy and from breast milk or formula. After six months, these stores start to become depleted and a source of iron should be introduced. Iron-fortified infant cereal contains about 7 mg per $\frac{1}{2}$ cup (125 mL) serving. One cup (250 mL), or 8 ounces, of iron-fortified infant formula contains about 5 mg.

Dietary Reference Intake for Iron

0 to 6 months	0.27 mg/day (AI)
7 to 12 months	11 mg/day (AI)
1 to 3 years	7 mg/day (AI)

Good sources of heme iron include beef, chicken and halibut. Good sources of non-heme iron include cream of wheat cereal, iron-fortified infant cereal, spinach, potatoes, beans, legumes, enriched white rice, prune juice and whole wheat bread.

Fat

Fat provides energy and plays a role in the absorption of the fat-soluble vitamins A, D, E and K. It also provides essential fatty acids that our bodies cannot produce on their own and helps insulate our bodies, protecting our vital organs.

All types of fat have the same amount of calories, but not all fats are created equal — some are more harmful to your health than others. **Saturated fat** and **trans fat** may increase a person's risk of heart disease, and experts believe that trans fat may carry an even greater health risk than saturated fat. **Monounsaturated fat** and **polyunsaturated fat** do not have the same negative effect on the heart.

Saturated and trans fats — such as butter, shortening or the fat on meat — are solid at room temperature. Saturated fat comes mostly from animal products, but some tropical oils, such as palm kernel oil and coconut oil, also contain saturated fat. Trans fat is also found in whole dairy and meat products. But one of the most common sources of trans fat in today's foods is hydrogenated vegetable oil. Hydrogenated oils are liquid oils that have been changed into a solid form of fat by adding hydrogen. This process allows these fats to keep for a long time without losing their flavor or going bad. Trans fats are often found in packaged baked goods such as cookies, crackers and potato chips. They are also present in fried foods such as french fries and doughnuts.

Unsaturated fats are liquid at room temperature. Unsaturated fats can be polyunsaturated or monounsaturated. Polyunsaturated fat is found in soybean, corn, sesame and sunflower oils, and fish and fish oil. Monounsaturated fat is found in avocados, olives, olive oil, canola oil, and most nuts and their oils.

Dietary Reference Intake for Total Fat

0 to 6 months	31 g/day (AI)
7 to 12 months	30 g/day (AI)
1 to 18 years	Insufficient scientific evidence was found to set an AI

Salt

It is not necessary to add salt to your toddler's diet. Children are not born with the desire for salty foods; this is a learned preference. Enough salt is found naturally in foods to satisfy the body's requirement.

Sugar

Adding sugar to your child's foods masks the natural taste, which children need to learn to like. Excess sugar leads to tooth decay and many unnecessary trips to the dentist.

Dealing with a Picky Eater

It is very common for toddlers to go through stages of likes and dislikes. Remember these important points when dealing with a picky eater:

- Fussy or picky eating is a normal part of growing up.
- Don't force your child to eat. Offer him a variety of healthy choices and let him choose how much he eats. This builds confidence!
- Let your child have his favorite food of the month over and over again as long as it is a healthy choice. He will grow out of it as time goes on.
- Introduce new foods regularly, and remember that it may take up to ten attempts to get a child to try a new food.
- Be patient with your child if he seems to dawdle at the table. He is learning a lot of new skills, like using utensils and cups.
- Make sure snacks are not served too close to mealtime. A hungry child is more likely to try new foods.
- Don't become a short-order cook. Children should choose from the foods that have been prepared, not demand that a new meal be cooked for them.
- Involve your child in meal preparation. He is more likely to try a food if he helped get it to the table.
- Lead by example. Let your child see you enjoying all the healthy choices you have prepared.

If a child is fussy or picky and is not growing properly, it is time to see your doctor.

FOOD FOR BABIES

Six Months and Older

Continued on next page…

Meal Plans

Continue breastfeeding or formula feeding on demand while you are introducing infant cereals, vegetables and fruits. Breast milk or formula is your child's best source of protein, fat and many vitamins and minerals, such as calcium. At this point, solid foods should be in addition to your regular breast milk or formula feedings. See the introduction for more information on these meal plans.

MEAL	1	2	3
Breakfast	• 2 tbsp (25 mL) prepared iron-fortified infant cereal • ¼ cup (50 mL) Apricots (page 27)	• 2 tbsp (25 mL) prepared iron-fortified infant cereal • ¼ cup (50 mL) Nectarines (page 34)	• 2 tbsp (25 mL) prepared iron-fortified infant cereal • ¼ cup (50 mL) Pears (page 36)
Snack	• Breast or formula feeding on demand	• Breast or formula feeding on demand	• Breast or formula feeding on demand
Lunch	• ¼ cup (50 mL) Sweet Potatoes (page 54)	• ¼ cup (50 mL) Squash (page 52)	• ¼ cup (50 mL) Parsnips (page 49)
Snack	• Breast or formula feeding on demand	• Breast or formula feeding on demand	• Breast or formula feeding on demand
Supper	• 2 tbsp (25 mL) prepared iron-fortified infant cereal • ¼ cup (50 mL) Apples (page 26)	• 2 tbsp (25 mL) prepared iron-fortified infant cereal • ¼ cup (50 mL) Squashed Green Beans (page 78)	• 2 tbsp (25 mL) prepared iron-fortified infant cereal • ¼ cup (50 mL) Broccoli Stems and Florets (page 42)
Snack	• Breast or formula feeding on demand	• Breast or formula feeding on demand	• Breast or formula feeding on demand

6

Apples are a good source of soluble fiber, which helps with bowel function and may lower cholesterol levels.

Apples

| 4 cups | chopped peeled apples (about 4) | 1 L |
| ½ cup | water | 125 mL |

1. In a medium saucepan, over medium-low heat, bring apples and water to a simmer, covered, stirring occasionally, until apples are very tender, about 20 minutes.

2. Transfer apples to blender and purée on high speed until smooth.

**Nutritional Information
(Per ¼-cup/50 mL Serving)**

Calories	12 Kcal
Total Carbohydrates	3 g
Fiber	1 g
Fat	0 g
Protein	0 g
Iron	0 mg

Apricots

2 cups	apricots	500 mL
¼ cup	water	50 mL

1. In a small saucepan of boiling water, blanch apricots for 30 seconds. Remove stones from apricots and chop.

2. Place in blender with ¼ cup (50 mL) water and purée on high speed until smooth.

**Nutritional Information
(Per ¼-cup/50 mL Serving)**

Calories..............................	18 Kcal
Total Carbohydrates.......................	4 g
Fiber	1 g
Fat	0 g
Protein	0 g
Iron	0 mg

**MAKES ABOUT
2 CUPS (500 ML)**

Apricots are very high in beta carotene and are an appetite stimulant. They have a stronger flavor than peaches and nectarines, so you may choose to dilute this purée with a bit of infant cereal when you first try it. If you're using dried apricots, be aware that they have mild laxative qualities.

TIP

Substitute dried apricots when fresh are not in season. Look for apricots that have not been treated with sulfites. Use 2 dried for each fresh apricot. Place dried apricots in a bowl and pour in boiling water to cover. Let sit for 30 minutes to rehydrate. Drain and blend according to recipe.

**MAKES ABOUT
½ CUP (125 ML)**

This "peel and mash" fruit is always quick, convenient and nutritious. Bananas are high in potassium and vitamin B$_6$.

TIP

Freeze chunks of unblemished bananas on a baking sheet in a single layer. When frozen, transfer to a resealable bag and freeze for up to 6 months. Purée until smooth to make a frozen banana treat.

Banana

1	very ripe banana	1

1. Place banana in blender and purée on high speed until smooth.

2. *Make ahead:* Store in an airtight container in the refrigerator for up to 1 day.

Nutritional Information (Per ¼-cup/50 mL Serving)	
Calories	80 Kcal
Total Carbohydrates	20 g
Fiber	2 g
Fat	0 g
Protein	1 g
Iron	0 mg

Blueberries

| 2 cups | blueberries (about 12 oz/375 g) | 500 mL |
| 1/2 cup | water | 125 mL |

1. In a medium saucepan, over medium heat, bring blueberries and water just to a boil. Cover, reduce heat and simmer for 15 minutes, until berries are very tender. Let cool.

2. Transfer blueberries to blender and purée on high speed until smooth.

3. Push through a fine sieve with a wooden spoon to remove any seeds that may be offensive to your baby.

Nutritional Information
(Per 1/4-cup/50 mL Serving)

Calories	20 Kcal
Total Carbohydrates	5 g
Fiber	1 g
Fat	0 g
Protein	0 g
Iron	0 mg

MAKES ABOUT 2 CUPS (500 ML)

Blueberries are fine to purée on high speed without cooking, but tend to be more tart that way.

TIP

Make up a batch of this recipe and blend a frozen cube of it (see introduction, page 14) with any fruit favorite, such as apples, pears or bananas.

MAKES 2 CUPS (500 ML)

Summer sweet cherries are the ultimate treat!

TIP

Cherries can be purchased already pitted and chilled, and can be portioned out and frozen to enjoy all year long.

Cherries

| 2 cups | pitted sweet red or black cherries (about 1 lb/500 g) | 500 mL |

1. Place cherries in blender and purée on high speed until smooth.

Nutritional Information (Per ¼-cup/50 mL Serving)

Calories	18 Kcal
Total Carbohydrates	4 g
Fiber	1 g
Fat	0 g
Protein	0 g
Iron	0 mg

MAKES ABOUT 2 CUPS (500 ML)

Kiwis are high in vitamins C and E and act as antioxidants. They have a rich, buttery texture that appeals to babies.

TIP

Choose kiwis that are firm but yield to gentle pressure. Place them in a brown paper bag to ripen.

Kiwi

| 3 cups | chopped peeled kiwis (about 6) | 750 mL |

1. Place kiwis in blender and purée on high speed until smooth.

2. *Make ahead:* Store in an airtight container in the refrigerator for up to 3 days. Do not freeze.

Nutritional Information (Per ¼-cup/50 mL Serving)

Calories	27 Kcal
Total Carbohydrates	7 g
Fiber	1 g
Fat	0 g
Protein	0 g
Iron	0 mg
Vitamin C	43 mg

Figs

2 cups	black figs, stems removed (about 8 oz/250 g)	500 mL
½ cup	water	125 mL

1. In a medium saucepan, over medium heat, bring figs and water just to a boil. Cover, reduce heat and simmer until figs are very tender, about 15 minutes. Let cool.

2. Transfer figs to blender and purée on high speed until smooth.

**Nutritional Information
(Per ¼-cup/50 mL Serving)**

Calories	37 Kcal
Total Carbohydrates	10 g
Fiber	2 g
Fat	0 g
Protein	0 g
Iron	0 mg

**MAKES ABOUT
2 CUPS (500 ML)**

Fresh figs are a good source of potassium and fiber; they also tend to have laxative properties.

TIP

If your baby is texture-sensitive, push the purée through a fine sieve with a wooden spoon to get a very smooth consistency.

Mangoes help the body maintain bowel regularity and fight infection. The skin can irritate a baby's mouth, so always peel.

TIP

Mangoes should have unblemished red and yellow skin that yields slightly to pressure. If mango is very fibrous, push puréed mango through a fine sieve with a wooden spoon to give a smooth, creamy consistency.

Mango

3 cups	chopped peeled mangoes (about 2 large)	750 mL
¼ cup	water	50 mL

1. Place mangoes and water in blender and purée on high speed until smooth.

**Nutritional Information
(Per ¼-cup/50 mL Serving)**

Calories	27 Kcal
Total Carbohydrates	7 g
Fiber	1 g
Fat	0 g
Protein	0 g
Iron	0 mg

The high water content of melons makes them very refreshing for little palates.

Watermelon

2½ cups	chopped seedless watermelon	375 mL

1. Place watermelon in blender and purée on high speed until smooth.

**Nutritional Information
(Per ¼-cup/50 mL Serving)**

Calories	15 Kcal
Total Carbohydrates	3 g
Fiber	0 g
Fat	0 g
Protein	0 g
Iron	0 mg

Papaya

3 cups	chopped peeled papaya (about 2)	750 mL
¼ cup	water	50 mL

1. Place papaya and water in blender and purée on high speed until smooth.

**Nutritional Information
(Per ¼-cup/50 mL Serving)**

Calories	20 Kcal
Total Carbohydrates	5 g
Fiber	1 g
Fat	0 g
Protein	0 g
Iron	0 mg
Vitamin C	32 mg

**MAKES ABOUT
2 CUPS (500 ML)**

Papaya is an excellent source of vitamin C and a good source of potassium and vitamin A.

TIP

Avoid papayas that are hard and green: they will be flavorless and will never ripen.

Melon

3 cups	cubed cantaloupe or honeydew melon (about ½)	750 mL

1. Place melon chunks in blender and purée on high speed until smooth.

**Nutritional Information
(Per ¼-cup/50 mL Serving)**

Calories	5 Kcal
Total Carbohydrates	1 g
Fiber	0 g
Fat	0 g
Protein	0 g
Iron	0 mg

**MAKES ABOUT
2 CUPS (500 ML)**

Melons are a good source of vitamin A and contain vitamin C and calcium. They have a mild, sweet flavor that appeals to babies.

TIP

Choose melons that are unblemished and heavy for their size and give off a fruity fragrance.

**MAKES ABOUT
2 CUPS (500 ML)**

Choose fruit that is heavy for its size — it will be full of juice. Nectarines should be firm, but not hard, with patches of red.

TIP

If you prefer to peel nectarines before puréeing, blanch them in boiling water for 30 seconds and transfer immediately to ice water. The peel will then come off easily with the tip of a sharp knife.

Nectarines

| 3 cups | chopped nectarines (about 4) | 750 mL |
| ¼ cup | water | 50 mL |

1. Place nectarines and water in blender and purée on high speed until smooth.

**Nutritional Information
(Per ¼-cup/50 mL Serving)**

Calories . . . . 17 Kcal
Total Carbohydrates . . . . 4 g
Fiber . . . . 1 g
Fat . . . . 0 g
Protein . . . . 0 g
Iron . . . . 0 mg

Peaches

| 4 | peaches | 4 |
| ½ cup | water | 125 mL |

1. In a small saucepan of boiling water, blanch peaches for 30 seconds. Plunge into cold water. Remove peel and stones from peaches and chop to make about 3 cups (750 mL).

2. Place in blender, add water and purée on high speed until smooth.

Nutritional Information (Per ¼-cup/50 mL Serving)	
Calories	18 Kcal
Total Carbohydrates	5 g
Fiber	1 g
Fat	0 g
Protein	0 g
Iron	0 mg

MAKES ABOUT 2 CUPS (500 ML)

Peaches spoil very easily, even when unripe, so buy only the quantity you are going to use and handle them with care, as they bruise easily. Store at room temperature until ready to use.

TIP

Substitute 3 cups (750 mL) frozen unsweetened sliced peaches if fresh are not available.

**MAKES ABOUT
2 CUPS (500 ML)**

*Pears are a sweet
source of soluble fiber.*

TIP

Very ripe pears can be
washed, peeled, cored,
chopped and processed
in the blender without
cooking.

Pears

| 3 cups | chopped peeled pears (about 4) | 750 mL |
| ½ cup | water | 125 mL |

1. In a medium saucepan, over medium-low heat,
   bring pears and water to a simmer, covered, stirring
   occasionally, until pears are very tender, about
   20 minutes. Let cool.

2. Transfer pears to blender and purée on high speed
   until smooth.

**Nutritional Information
(Per ¼-cup/50 mL Serving)**

Calories. . . . . 24 Kcal
Total Carbohydrates . . . . .6 g
Fiber . . . . .1 g
Fat . . . . .0 g
Protein . . . . .0 g
Iron . . . . 0 mg

Plums

| 3 cups | chopped plums (about 6) | 750 mL |
| 1/2 cup | water | 125 mL |

1. In a medium saucepan, over medium-low heat, bring plums and water to a simmer, covered, stirring occasionally, until plums are very tender, about 20 minutes. Let cool.

2. Transfer plums to blender and purée on high speed until smooth.

**Nutritional Information
(Per 1/4-cup/50 mL Serving)**

Calories	23 Kcal
Total Carbohydrates	5 g
Fiber	1 g
Fat	0 g
Protein	0 g
Iron	0 mg

**MAKES ABOUT
2 CUPS (500 ML)**

Like prunes and apricots, plums have laxative properties. They are excellent stewed, as in this recipe, or puréed fresh when they are ripe and sweet.

TIP

Look for plums with a powdery "bloom" on them; it's a sign that they haven't been handled too much.

*These natural laxatives
should be used in
moderation unless
constipation is an issue.*

TIP

If your baby is
texture-sensitive,
push the purée
through a fine sieve
with a wooden spoon
to get a very smooth
consistency.

Prunes

| 1 ½ cups | pitted prunes (about 8 oz/250 g) | 375 mL |
| ½ cup | water | 125 mL |

1. In a medium saucepan, over medium heat, bring
prunes and water just to a boil. Cover, reduce heat
and simmer until prunes are very tender, about
15 minutes. Let cool.

2. Transfer prunes to blender and purée on high speed
until smooth.

**Nutritional Information
(Per ¼-cup/50 mL Serving)**

Calories	75 Kcal
Total Carbohydrates	20 g
Fiber	2 g
Fat	0 g
Protein	1 g
Iron	0 mg

Strawberries, Raspberries or Blackberries

| 2 cups | fresh raspberries, blackberries or sliced strawberries | 500 mL |
| ½ cup | water | 125 mL |

1. Place berries and water in blender and purée on high speed until smooth.

2. Push through a fine sieve with a wooden spoon to remove any seeds.

**Nutritional Information
(Per ¼-cup/50 mL Serving)**

Raspberries
Calories . . . . 16 Kcal
Total Carbohydrates . . . . 4 g
Fiber . . . . 2 g
Fat . . . . 0 g
Protein . . . . 0 g
Iron . . . . 0 mg

Blackberries
Calories . . . . 19 Kcal
Total Carbohydrates . . . . 5 g
Fiber . . . . 2 g
Fat . . . . 0 g
Protein . . . . 0 g
Iron . . . . 0 mg

Strawberries
Calories . . . . 11 Kcal
Total Carbohydrates . . . . 3 g
Fiber . . . . 1 g
Fat . . . . 0 g
Protein . . . . 0 g
Iron . . . . 0 mg
Vitamin C . . . . 21 mg

**MAKES ABOUT
2 CUPS (500 ML)**

Berries are sometimes hard on little tummies. Try berries when baby has tried many of the other fruits and vegetables and the digestive tract is more developed. Make sure to watch for a reaction.

TIP

Use an equal amount of frozen berries when fresh are not in season.

Avocado is high in essential fats that are necessary for proper growth and development. They can be eaten right out of the skin and have a buttery texture that babies love!

TIP

Avocados oxidize and turn gray very quickly after slicing, so it's best to use up this purée as soon as it's made.

Avocado

| ¼ cup | chopped peeled avocado (about ½) | 50 mL |

1. Place avocado in blender and purée on high speed until smooth.

**Nutritional Information
(Per ¼-cup/50 mL Serving)**

Calories. . . . . 59 Kcal
Total Carbohydrates . . . . 3 g
Fiber . . . . 1 g
Fat . . . . 6 g
Protein . . . . 1 g
Iron . . . . 0 mg

Beets

2 cups	chopped peeled beets (about 1 bunch)	500 mL
½ cup	water	125 mL

1. In a medium saucepan, over medium heat, bring beets and water just to a boil. Cover, reduce heat and simmer until very tender, about 20 minutes. Let cool.

2. Transfer beets to blender and purée on high speed until smooth.

Nutritional Information
(Per ¼-cup/50 mL Serving)

Calories	15 Kcal
Total Carbohydrates	1 g
Fiber	1 g
Fat	0 g
Protein	1 g
Iron	0 mg

**MAKES ABOUT
2 CUPS (500 ML)**

Beets are very easily digested and stimulate the appetite. Be aware that beets will often discolor urine and stools, but this should not be cause for concern.

**MAKES ABOUT
2 CUPS (500 ML)**

*Cooked broccoli is
an excellent source
of vitamin C and
potassium.*

TIPS

Use a vegetable peeler
to remove the fibrous
skin from broccoli
stems.

Once your baby is
used to the flavor of
broccoli, use the same
cooking method with
2½ cups (625 mL)
florets (the texture
of the buds can be
off-putting to younger
children).

Broccoli Stems and Florets

| 1½ cups | sliced peeled broccoli stems (see tips, at left) | 375 mL |
| 1 cup | water | 250 mL |

1. In a medium saucepan, over medium heat, bring
stems and water to a boil. Cover, reduce heat
and simmer until broccoli is very tender, about
15 minutes. Let cool.

2. Transfer broccoli to blender and purée on high
speed until smooth.

**Nutritional Information
(Per ¼-cup/50 mL Serving)**

Calories . . . . 8 Kcal
Total Carbohydrates . . . . 1 g
Fiber . . . . 0 g
Fat: . . . . 0 g
Protein . . . . 1 g
Iron . . . . 0 mg
Vitamin C . . . . 26 mg

Cabbage

3 cups	chopped cabbage (about 8 oz/250 g)	750 mL

1. Place cabbage in a steamer basket fitted over a saucepan of boiling water; cover and steam for 15 to 20 minutes, or until very tender. Let cool.

2. Transfer cabbage to blender and purée on high speed, adding water if necessary, until smooth.

Nutritional Information
(Per ¼-cup/50 mL Serving)

Calories	8 Kcal
Total Carbohydrates	2 g
Fiber	1 g
Fat	0 g
Protein	0 g
Iron	0 mg

MAKES ABOUT 2 CUPS (500 ML)

Green, red, Savoy, Napa and bok choy are some of the different varieties of this nutrient-dense vegetable. They can all be prepared in the same manner.

**MAKES ABOUT
2 CUPS (500 ML)**

*Carrots are naturally
sweet and very
nutritious. Cooking
carrots maximizes their
nutritional potential
and flavor.*

TIP

The green tops draw
nutrients from the
carrots. Choose carrots
that have them
removed, or remove
them immediately
after purchasing.

Carrots

| 2 cups | chopped peeled carrots (about 4) | 500 mL |
| 1 cup | water | 125 mL |

1. In a medium saucepan, over medium heat, bring carrots and water just to a boil. Cover, reduce heat and simmer until carrots are very tender, about 15 minutes. Let cool.

2. Transfer carrots to blender and purée on high speed until smooth.

**Nutritional Information
(Per ¼-cup/50 mL Serving)**

Calories. . . . . 14 Kcal
Total Carbohydrates . . . . 3 g
Fiber . . . . 1 g
Fat . . . . 0 g
Protein . . . . 0 g
Iron . . . . 0 mg

Cauliflower

| 1 ½ cups | cauliflower florets | 375 mL |
| 1 cup | water | 250 mL |

1. In a medium saucepan, over medium heat, bring cauliflower and water just to a boil. Cover, reduce heat and simmer until cauliflower is very tender, about 10 minutes. Let cool.

2. Transfer cauliflower to blender and purée on high speed until smooth.

Nutritional Information (Per ¼-cup/50 mL Serving)	
Calories	8 Kcal
Total Carbohydrates	2 g
Fiber	1 g
Fat	0 g
Protein	0 g
Iron	0 mg

MAKES ABOUT 2 CUPS (500 ML)

Cauliflower is the most easily digestible member of the cabbage family and is a great introduction to the cruciferous group, which also includes cabbage, broccoli, Brussels sprouts, collard greens and kohlrabi.

TIP

Add a piece of bread to the water when boiling to absorb some of the odor. Discard bread before puréeing.

**MAKES 2 CUPS
(500 ML)**

Purchase fresh corn still in its husk, as it perishes very quickly. The silk should feel moist, and the kernels should be firm and should produce a milky juice when pierced. Shuck the corn and remove the kernels by running a sharp knife along the cob. Use immediately.

TIP

Substitute frozen kernels when fresh are not in season.

Corn

2 cups	fresh or frozen corn kernels	500 mL
1/2 cup	water	125 mL

1. In a medium saucepan, over medium heat, bring corn and water just to a boil. Cover, reduce heat and simmer until corn is tender, about 3 minutes. Let cool.

2. Transfer corn to blender and purée on high speed until smooth.

**Nutritional Information
(Per 1/4-cup/50 mL Serving)**

Calories. . . . . 49 Kcal
Total Carbohydrates. . . . . 12 g
Fiber . . . . 1 g
Fat . . . . 0 g
Protein . . . . 2 g
Iron . . . . 0 mg

**MAKES ABOUT
1 CUP (250 ML)**

Cucumber is very mild and refreshing. The waxy skin is not very palatable for little ones, so always peel before using.

MAKE AHEAD

Store in an airtight container in the refrigerator for up to 3 days. Do not freeze.

Cucumber

1 1/2 cups	cubed peeled and seeded cucumber (about 1 small)	375 mL

1. Place in blender and purée on high speed until smooth.

**Nutritional Information
(Per 1/4-cup/50 mL Serving)**

Calories. . . . . 7 Kcal
Total Carbohydrates. . . . . 2 g
Fiber . . . . 0 g
Fat . . . . 0 g
Protein . . . . 0 g
Iron . . . . 0 mg

Green Beans

| 3 cups | halved trimmed green beans (about 12 oz/375 g) | 750 mL |
| 2 cups | water | 500 mL |

1. In a large saucepan, over medium-high heat, bring beans and water to a boil. Cover, reduce heat and simmer until beans are very tender, about 15 minutes. Let cool.

2. Transfer beans to blender and purée on high speed until smooth.

Nutritional Information
(Per ¼-cup/50 mL Serving)

Calories	13 Kcal
Total Carbohydrates	3 g
Fiber	1 g
Fat	0 g
Protein	1 g
Iron	0 mg

MAKES ABOUT 2 CUPS (500 ML)

Choose young green beans that are tender and not too fibrous, and remove any fibers that are on them. French beans make the smoothest purée.

TIPS

Substitute frozen green beans if fresh are not available.

If your baby is texture-sensitive, push the purée through a fine sieve with a wooden spoon to get a very smooth consistency.

Beet greens, collard greens, mustard greens, kale and Swiss chard all fall into this group, and all are excellent sources of vitamin A.

Dark Leafy Greens

| 6 cups | chopped dark leafy greens, tough stems and ribs removed | 1.5 L |
| ½ cup | water | 125 mL |

1. Arrange greens in a large nonstick skillet. Pour in water, cover and cook over medium-high heat, stirring occasionally, until greens are very tender, about 15 minutes. Let cool.

2. Transfer greens to blender and purée on high speed, adding water if necessary, until smooth.

**Nutritional Information
(Per ¼-cup/50 mL Serving)**

Calories . . . . 34 Kcal
Total Carbohydrates . . . . 7 g
Fiber . . . . 1 g
Fat . . . . 0 g
Protein . . . . 2 g
Iron . . . . 1 mg
Vitamin C . . . . 80 mg

Parsnips

| 2 cups | chopped peeled parsnips (about 4) | 500 mL |
| 1 cup | water | 250 mL |

1. In a medium saucepan, over medium heat, bring parsnips and water just to a boil. Cover, reduce heat and simmer until very tender, about 20 minutes. Let cool.

2. Transfer parsnips to blender and purée on high speed until smooth.

**Nutritional Information
(Per ¼-cup/50 mL Serving)**

Calories	25 Kcal
Total Carbohydrates	6 g
Fiber	2 g
Fat	0 g
Protein	0 g
Iron	0 mg

**MAKES 2 CUPS
(500 ML)**

Like many other root vegetables, parsnips have a mild, sweet flavor that infants love.

TIP

Choose parsnips that are small and firm; larger, older parsnips have a higher starch content that may produce a purée that is too sticky once blended

Pumpkin

**MAKES ABOUT
2 CUPS (500 ML)**

Pumpkin is a nice change from squash and has a flavor that babies love.

TIP

Dice extra pumpkin and freeze in a single layer on a baking sheet covered with plastic wrap. Once completely frozen, transfer to a resealable bag for use throughout the year.

| 3 cups | cubed peeled pie pumpkin | 750 mL |
| 1 cup | water | 250 mL |

1. In a large saucepan, over medium-high heat, bring pumpkin and water to a boil. Cover, reduce heat and simmer until pumpkin is very tender, about 25 minutes. Let cool.

2. Transfer pumpkin and cooking liquid to blender and purée on high speed until smooth.

**Nutritional Information
(Per ¼-cup/50 mL Serving)**

Calories	8 Kcal
Total Carbohydrates	2 g
Fiber	0 g
Fat	0 g
Protein	0 g
Iron	0 mg

Spinach

4 cups	lightly packed fresh spinach leaves (about 3 oz/90 g)	1 L
½ cup	water	125 mL

1. Wash spinach leaves thoroughly in a basin of cold water, changing water often. Remove tough stems and ribs and roughly chop leaves.

2. Arrange spinach in a large nonstick skillet. Pour in water, cover and cook over medium-high heat, stirring occasionally, until wilted and bright green, about 5 minutes. Let cool.

3. Transfer spinach to blender and purée on high speed until smooth.

Nutritional Information
(Per ¼-cup/50 mL Serving)

Calories	3 Kcal
Total Carbohydrates	1 g
Fiber	0 g
Fat	0 g
Protein	0 g
Iron	0 mg

**MAKES ABOUT
2 CUPS (500 ML)**

Wash spinach very well and don't overcook it — overcooking can bring out its bitterness. Old, tough leaves should be avoided.

TIPS

Substitute frozen spinach when fresh is not available.

Spinach can also be used raw if using tender baby spinach leaves.

In autumn, any variety of squash makes an ideal beginner purée.

TIP

Use diced frozen squash when fresh is not in season or when you're in a hurry.

Squash

| 3 cups | cubed peeled butternut or acorn squash | 750 mL |
| 1 cup | water | 250 mL |

1. In a medium saucepan, over medium-high heat, bring squash and water to a boil. Cover, reduce heat and simmer until squash is very tender, about 20 minutes. Let cool.

2. Transfer squash to blender and purée on high speed until smooth.

**Nutritional Information
(Per ¼-cup/50 mL Serving)**

Calories . . . . 12 Kcal
Total Carbohydrates . . . . 3 g
Fiber . . . . 0 g
Fat . . . . 0 g
Protein . . . . 0 g
Iron . . . . 0 mg

Sweet Peas

| 3 cups | fresh or frozen sweet peas | 750 mL |
| 2 cups | water | 500 mL |

1. In a large saucepan, over medium-high heat, bring peas and water to a boil. Cover, reduce heat and simmer for 5 minutes, until peas are tender. Let cool.

2. Transfer peas to blender and purée on high speed until smooth.

**Nutritional Information
(Per ¼-cup/50 mL Serving)**

Calories	42 Kcal
Total Carbohydrates	7 g
Fiber	3 g
Fat	0 g
Protein	3 g
Iron	1 mg

**MAKES ABOUT
2 CUPS (500 ML)**

If shelling peas isn't quite the labor of love you were looking for, frozen peas offer the same nutritional value without the work

TIP

If your baby is texture-sensitive, push the purée through a fine sieve with a wooden spoon to get a very smooth consistency

53

*Sweet potatoes, carrots,
mangoes and other
orange fruits and
vegetables are high in
beta carotene, which
the body converts to
vitamin A. Vitamin A
is important for
vision, bone growth,
reproduction and
cell division.*

Sweet Potatoes

3 cups	cubed peeled sweet potatoes (about 2)	750 mL
1 cup	water	250 mL

1. In a medium saucepan, over medium-high heat,
   bring potatoes and water to a boil. Cover, reduce
   heat and simmer until potatoes are very tender,
   about 20 minutes. Let cool.

2. Transfer potatoes to blender and purée on high
   speed until smooth.

**Nutritional Information
(Per ¼-cup/50 mL Serving)**

Calories . . . . 26 Kcal
Total Carbohydrates . . . . 6 g
Fiber . . . . 1 g
Fat . . . . 0 g
Protein . . . . 0 g
Iron . . . . 0 mg

Turnips

2 cups	chopped peeled white turnips (about 4)	500 mL
1 cup	water	250 mL

1. In a medium saucepan, over medium-high heat, bring turnips and water to a boil. Cover, reduce heat and simmer until turnips are very tender, about 15 minutes. Let cool.

2. Transfer turnips to blender and purée on high speed until smooth.

Nutritional Information
(Per ¼-cup/50 mL Serving)

Calories	9 Kcal
Total Carbohydrates	2 g
Fiber	1 g
Fat	0 g
Protein	0 g
Iron	0 mg

MAKES ABOUT 2 CUPS (500 ML)

Turnips are purplish white root vegetables that are similar in size to beets. In North America, we often refer to rutabagas as turnips, but rutabagas are large, yellow-fleshed, waxy vegetables that are harder on babies' stomachs.

*Choose zucchini and
yellow squash that are
small and have thin,
unblemished skin; they
are the most tender
and have a sweet
mild flavor.*

TIP

Scrub zucchini well and
cut off both ends, but
do not peel: the rind
offers both nutrients
and a delightful pale
green color!

Zucchini/Yellow Squash

3 cups	sliced zucchini or yellow squash (about 2)	750 mL

1. Place zucchini in a steaming basket fitted over a saucepan of boiling water, cover and steam for 15 minutes, or until very tender. Let cool.

2. Transfer zucchini to blender and purée on high speed until smooth.

**Nutritional Information
(Per ¼-cup/50 mL Serving)**

Calories	5 Kcal
Total Carbohydrates	1 g
Fiber	0 g
Fat	0 g
Protein	0 g
Iron	0 mg

Cranberry Apple Mush

4 cups	sliced peeled apples (about 3 large)	1 L
½ cup	fresh or frozen cranberries	125 mL
½ cup	sweetened apple juice	125 mL
1 tsp	ground cinnamon	5 mL

1. In a medium saucepan, over medium-high heat, bring apples, cranberries, apple juice and cinnamon to a boil. Cover, reduce heat and simmer until apples are very tender, about 25 minutes. Let cool.

2. Transfer to blender and purée on high speed until smooth.

Nutritional Information
(Per ¼-cup/50 mL Serving)

Calories	44 Kcal
Total Carbohydrates	11 g
Fiber	2 g
Fat	0 g
Protein	0 g
Iron	0 mg

MAKES ABOUT 2 CUPS (500 ML)

Everyday apples get some zip from tart autumn cranberries.

TIP

Cranberries are known to be effective in preventing urinary tract infections.

*A deep orange color is
generally an indication
that the fruit or
vegetable contains
beta carotene and
vitamin C — this is
a triple dose, packed
with flavor!*

TIP

Substitute additional
water for the orange
juice for young
stomachs that are
irritated by citrus.

FOR OLDER KIDS

Add a dash of curry
powder and 2 cups
(500 mL) vegetable or
chicken stock while
cooking to make a
delicious soup. Serve
with warm whole-grain
rolls.

Orange, Orange, Orange

1 cup	diced peeled carrots (about 2)	250 mL
1 cup	diced peeled sweet potato (about ½)	250 mL
½ cup	diced peeled pear (about ½)	125 mL
½ cup	orange juice (see tip, at left)	125 mL
½ cup	water	125 mL

1. In a medium saucepan, over medium-high heat,
   bring carrots, sweet potato, pear, orange juice and
   water to a boil. Cover, reduce heat and simmer
   until vegetables are very tender, about 20 minutes.
   Let cool.

2. Transfer to blender with cooking liquid and purée
   on high speed, adding more water if necessary,
   until smooth.

**Nutritional Information
(Per ¼-cup/50 mL Serving)**

Calories. . . . . 71 Kcal
Total Carbohydrates . . . . 12 g
Fiber . . . . 1 g
Fat . . . . 2 g
Protein . . . . 1 g
Iron . . . . 0 mg

Cherried Peaches

2 cups	sliced peeled peaches (about 3)	500 mL
1 cup	pitted red sour cherries (about 8 oz/250 g)	250 mL
½ cup	peach nectar	125 mL

1. In blender, combine peaches, cherries and peach nectar and purée on high speed until smooth.

Nutritional Information (Per ¼-cup/50 mL Serving)	
Calories	36 Kcal
Total Carbohydrates	9 g
Fiber	1 g
Fat	0 g
Protein	1 g
Iron	0 mg

MAKES ABOUT 2 CUPS (500 ML)

Summer fruits are combined in this quick and easy dessert.

TIP

Buy pitted cherries during the summer and keep them portioned in your freezer for easy use throughout the year.

FOR OLDER KIDS

Freeze mixture in ice-pop molds for a

Peach-Pear Bananarama

1½ cups	diced peeled peaches (about 2)	375 mL
1 cup	diced peeled pear (about 1)	250 mL
1	banana, sliced	1

1. In blender, combine peaches, pear and banana and purée on high speed until smooth.

Nutritional Information (Per ¼-cup/50 mL Serving)	
Calories	29 Kcal
Total Carbohydrates	7 g
Fiber	1 g
Fat	0 g
Protein	0 g
Iron	0 mg

MAKES ABOUT 3 CUPS (750 ML)

FOR OLDER KIDS

For a special treat, stir this purée into their favorite porridge with a sprinkle of ground cinnamon.

6

*Figs are a good source
of potassium and fiber;
paired with the mild,
sweet taste of pears
(which are also a good
source of soluble fiber),
this purée is a great
spread for adults too!*

Figgy Pears

1½ cups	diced peeled pears (about 2)	375 mL
¾ cup	unsweetened orange juice	175 mL
½ cup	diced figs, stems removed (about 4 oz/125 g)	125 mL
¼ tsp	ground allspice	1 mL

1. In a medium saucepan, over medium-low heat, combine pears, orange juice, figs and allspice. Bring to a simmer, cover and cook until pears and figs are very tender, about 20 minutes. Let cool.

2. Transfer to blender and purée on high speed until smooth.

**Nutritional Information
(Per ¼-cup/50 mL Serving)**

Calories	44 Kcal
Total Carbohydrates	11 g
Fiber	1 g
Fat	0 g
Protein	0 g
Iron	0 mg

Purple Pears

1 cup	diced peeled beets (about 2)	250 mL
1 cup	diced peeled pear (about 1)	250 mL
½ cup	unsweetened apple juice	125 mL

1. In a medium saucepan, over low heat, combine beets, pear and apple juice. Bring to a simmer, cover and cook until beets and pears are very tender, about 30 minutes. Let cool.

2. Transfer to blender with cooking liquid and purée on high speed until smooth.

Nutritional Information (Per ¼-cup/50 mL Serving)	
Calories	27 Kcal
Total Carbohydrates	7 g
Fiber	1 g
Fat	0 g
Protein	0 g
Iron	0 mg

**MAKES ABOUT
2 CUPS (500 ML)**

The color alone makes this worth making! This smooth, deep purple purée is sure to be a hit, and will be added to your baby's growing repertoire of veggie favorites. Be aware that beets will often discolor urine and stools, but this is not a cause for concern.

TIPS

Avoid buying elongated beets — they are more fibrous and do not provide a smooth-textured purée

Use gloves when peeling beets so you don't stain your hands (but lemon juice does the trick in removing the stains if you forget).

**MAKES ABOUT
2 CUPS (500 ML)**

*Blended melon flavors
combine in a refreshing
treat for your baby.*

TIPS

To peel melons: Cut
in half and reserve
one half for later use.
Cut the other half
lengthwise into four
wedges. Peel the
wedges and discard
seeds, if any.

Choose melons that
are unblemished,
fragrant and heavy
for their size.

FOR OLDER KIDS

Freeze unused chopped
peeled melon in an
airtight container in
the freezer. In blender,
combine 1 cup (250 mL)
frozen melon pieces
and purée on high
speed until smooth
for an icy treat.

Melon Madness

1 cup	diced cantaloupe	250 mL
1 cup	diced honeydew melon	250 mL
1 cup	diced seedless watermelon	250 mL

1. In blender, combine cantaloupe, honeydew and
watermelon and purée on high speed until smooth.

**Nutritional Information
(Per ¼-cup/50 mL Serving)**

Calories	21 Kcal
Total Carbohydrates	5 g
Fiber	0 g
Fat	0 g
Protein	0 g
Iron	0 mg

Watermelon Refresher

2 cups	diced seedless watermelon	500 mL
½ cup	diced peeled kiwi (about 1)	125 mL
½ cup	sliced strawberries	125 mL
1 tbsp	lime juice	15 mL

1. In blender, combine watermelon, kiwi, strawberries and lime juice and purée on high speed until smooth.

Nutritional Information
(Per ¼-cup/50 mL Serving)

Calories	22 Kcal
Total Carbohydrates	5 g
Fiber	1 g
Fat	0 g
Protein	0 g
Iron	0 mg

MAKES ABOUT 2 CUPS (500 ML)

Watermelon blends well with other fruits to make a naturally sweet thirst quencher.

TIP

Use an equal amount of frozen strawberries when fresh are not in season.

FOR OLDER KIDS

Freeze purée in ice-pop molds for a frosty treat.

6

TIP

Use an equal amount
of frozen berries when
fresh are not in season.

Rhubarb, Apples and Berries

2 cups	sliced peeled apples (about 2)	500 mL
1 cup	chopped rhubarb (about 2 stalks)	250 mL
1/4 cup	raspberries and/or blueberries	50 mL
1/4 cup	frozen apple juice concentrate	50 mL

1. In a medium saucepan, over medium-low heat, combine apples, rhubarb, berries and apple juice concentrate. Bring to a simmer, cover and cook, stirring occasionally, until fruit is very tender, about 30 minutes. Let cool.

2. Transfer to blender and purée on high speed until smooth.

Nutritional Information (Per 1/4-cup/50 mL Serving)	
Calories	36 Kcal
Total Carbohydrates	9 g
Fiber	1 g
Fat	0 g
Protein	0 g
Iron	0 mg

Strawberry Decadence

1 cup	fresh or frozen strawberries	250 mL
1 cup	sliced apricots (2 to 3)	250 mL
	Zest and juice of 1 lemon	

1. In blender, combine strawberries, apricots, and lemon zest and juice and purée on high speed until smooth.

2. *Make ahead:* Store in an airtight container in the refrigerator for up to 1 week.

**Nutritional Information
(Per ¼-cup/50 mL Serving)**

Calories . . . . 17 Kcal
Total Carbohydrates . . . . 4 g
Fiber . . . . 1 g
Fat . . . . 0 g
Protein . . . . 0 g
Iron . . . . 0 mg

**MAKES ABOUT
2 CUPS (500 ML)**

Creamy apricots make this strawberry purée an absolute delight!

TIPS

Apricots are an excellent source of Vitamin A. When fresh are not in season, used dried that have been rehydrated in boiling water for 30 minutes, or until swollen and softened. Use liquid with apricots.

Serve this over angel food cake topped with vanilla ice cream… yum! Who said baby food wasn't for everyone?

FOR OLDER KIDS

To make a great smoothie, add ½ cup (125 mL) milk to 1 cup (250 mL) of the purée.

Tropical Fruit Breeze

1 cup	chopped peeled kiwi (about 2)	250 mL
½ cup	sliced banana (about 1 small)	125 mL
½ cup	chopped peeled mango (about ½)	125 mL
½ cup	orange juice	125 mL

1. In blender, combine kiwi, banana, mango and orange juice and purée on high speed until smooth.

2. *Make ahead:* Store in an airtight container in the refrigerator for up to 5 days.

**Nutritional Information
(Per ½-cup/125 mL Serving)**

Calories. . . . . 107 Kcal
Total Carbohydrates. . . . . 27 g
Fiber . . . . 3 g
Fat . . . . 1 g
Protein . . . . 1 g
Iron . . . . 0 mg
Vitamin C. . . . . 54 mg

Avocado, Mango and Lime

½ cup	diced peeled avocado (about ½)	125 mL
½ cup	diced peeled mango (about ½)	125 mL
2 tbsp	freshly squeezed lime juice	25 mL

1. In blender, combine avocado, mango and lime juice and purée on high speed until smooth.

2. *Make ahead:* Store in an airtight container in the refrigerator for up to 1 day.

Nutritional Information
(Per ¼-cup/50 mL Serving)

Calories	44 Kcal
Total Carbohydrates	5 g
Fiber	1 g
Fat	3 g
Protein	0 g
Iron	0 mg

**MAKES ABOUT
1 CUP (500 ML)**

TIPS

Avocados offer more protein than any other fruit and are high in essential fatty acids, ideal for baby's development.

Prevent discoloration of the avocado's flesh by sprinkling it with lemon or lime juice.

**MAKES ABOUT
3 CUPS (375 ML)**

Baking the apples and squash maximizes their flavor and brings their natural sugars to life.

FOR OLDER KIDS

Put $1/2$ cup (125 mL) squashed apples in a ramekin. Toss $1/4$ cup (50 mL) granola cereal with 1 tbsp (15 mL) melted butter and sprinkle over top. Bake in oven preheated to 350°F (180°C) until granola is golden, about 12 minutes.

VARIATION

Omit oil and syrup and combine apples, squash, nutmeg and apple juice in a medium saucepan over medium heat. Bring to a simmer, cover and cook until very tender, about 20 minutes; purée on high speed in blender until smooth.

Squashed Apples

Preheat oven to 350°F (180°C)
Rimmed baking sheet, lined with foil

2 cups	diced peeled butternut squash	500 mL
1 cup	diced peeled Golden Delicious apple (about 1)	250 mL
1 tbsp	vegetable oil	15 mL
1 tsp	pure maple syrup	5 mL
Pinch	ground nutmeg	Pinch
$1/2$ cup	unsweetened apple juice or water	125 mL

1. In a medium bowl, toss squash and apple with oil, maple syrup and nutmeg.

2. Spread on prepared baking sheet and bake in preheated oven until apples and squash are tender and golden, about 30 minutes. Let cool.

3. In blender, combine apple mixture and apple juice and purée on high speed until smooth.

**Nutritional Information
(Per $1/4$-cup/50 mL Serving)**

Calories . . . . 46 Kcal
Total Carbohydrates . . . . 8 g
Fiber . . . . 1 g
Fat . . . . 2 g
Protein . . . . 0 g
Iron . . . . 0 mg

Carrots and Dates

2 cups	sliced peeled carrots (about 4)	500 mL
1 cup	unsweetened apple juice or water	250 mL
½ cup	chopped pitted dates (about 3 oz/90 g)	125 mL

1. In a medium saucepan, over medium-high heat, bring carrots, apple juice and dates to a boil. Cover, reduce heat and simmer until carrots are very tender, about 15 minutes. Let cool.

2. Transfer to blender and purée on high speed until smooth.

Nutritional Information
(Per ¼-cup/50 mL Serving)

Calories	52 Kcal
Total Carbohydrates	13 g
Fiber	1 g
Fat	0 g
Protein	0 g
Iron	0 mg

MAKES ABOUT 2 CUPS (500 ML)

Dates lend sweetness and fiber to a favorite vegetable!

TIP

Use this as a spread on whole-grain toast and bran muffins for the whole family.

TIP

Use an equal amount of frozen raspberries when fresh are not in season.

Carrots with Apricots and Berries

1 cup	diced peeled carrots (about 2)	250 mL
1 cup	sliced pitted apricots (2 to 3)	250 mL
½ cup	raspberries	125 mL

1. Place carrots in a steaming basket fitted over a saucepan of boiling water; cover and steam until very tender, about 15 minutes. Let cool.

2. In blender, combine carrots, apricots and raspberries; purée on high speed until smooth. Pass through a fine sieve with a wooden spoon to remove seeds.

**Nutritional Information
(Per ¼-cup/50 mL Serving)**

Calories . . . . 20 Kcal
Total Carbohydrates . . . . 5 g
Fiber . . . . 1 g
Fat . . . . 0 g
Protein . . . . 1 g
Iron . . . . 0 mg

Pears, Carrots and Squash

1 cup	diced peeled butternut squash	250 mL
1 cup	sliced peeled pear (about 1)	250 mL
½ cup	sliced peeled carrot (about 1)	125 mL
¼ cup	unsweetened apple juice or water	50 mL

1. In a medium saucepan, over medium heat, combine squash, pear, carrot and apple juice. Bring to a simmer, cover and cook until all are very tender, about 20 minutes. Let cool.

2. Transfer to blender and purée on high speed until smooth.

**Nutritional Information
(Per ¼-cup/50 mL Serving)**

Calories	24 Kcal
Total Carbohydrates	6 g
Fiber	1 g
Fat	0 g
Protein	0 g
Iron	0 mg

**MAKES ABOUT
2 CUPS (500 ML)**

Combining fruits and veggies is a great way to pack nutrients into simple purées.

MAKES ABOUT 2 CUPS (500 ML)

Pumpkin has more flavor than other varieties of winter squash; it's a nice alternative when in season.

TIPS

Do not substitute canned pie filling, which has additives in it, for the pumpkin.

Cut peeled and seeded pumpkin into chunks and freeze in a resealable bag for up to 6 months.

Orange Pumpkin Purée

Preheat oven to 350°F (180°C)
Rimmed baking sheet, lined with foil

2 cups	cubed peeled pie pumpkin	500 mL
1 tbsp	vegetable oil	15 mL
1 tsp	ground cinnamon	5 mL
Pinch	ground allspice	Pinch
1/2 cup	orange juice	125 mL

1. In a medium bowl, toss pumpkin with vegetable oil, cinnamon and allspice.

2. Arrange in a single layer on prepared baking sheet and bake in preheated oven until pumpkin is golden and tender, about 30 minutes. Let cool slightly.

3. Transfer to blender, add orange juice and purée on high speed until smooth.

**Nutritional Information
(Per 1/4-cup/50 mL Serving)**

Calories . . . . 30 Kcal
Total Carbohydrates . . . . 4 g
Fiber . . . . 0 g
Fat . . . . 2 g
Protein . . . . 0 g
Iron . . . . 0 mg

Pumpkin and Apples

2 cups	cubed peeled apples (about 2)	500 mL
1 cup	diced peeled pie pumpkin	250 mL
½ cup	unsweetened apple juice	125 mL
1 tsp	vanilla	5 mL
½ tsp	ground cinnamon	2 mL

1. In a medium saucepan, over medium-low heat, combine apples, pumpkin, apple juice, vanilla and cinnamon. Cover and simmer until apples and pumpkin are very tender, about 30 minutes. Let cool.

2. Transfer to blender and purée on high speed until smooth.

Nutritional Information
(Per ¼-cup/50 mL Serving)

Calories	22 Kcal
Total Carbohydrates	5 g
Fiber	1 g
Fat	0 g
Protein	1 g
Iron	0 mg

**MAKES ABOUT
2 CUPS (500 ML)**

These two fall favorites have mild, slightly sweet flavors that taste great together.

TIP

Pie pumpkins are sold in the autumn and usually weigh 1 to 3 lbs (500 g to 1.5 kg). They have a sweeter flavor and are less fibrous than the larger varieties sold for carving.

*This silky-smooth
purée just might
convert babies who
don't like squash!*

TIP

For a simpler method,
and a milder flavor,
omit the oil and cook
the squash, pears,
rosemary and water in
a medium saucepan
over medium heat
until very tender, about
20 minutes. Purée on
high speed as in Step 3.

Roasted Squash and Pears

Preheat oven to 400°F (200°C)
Rimmed baking sheet, lined with foil

1 ½ cups	cubed peeled butternut squash	375 mL
1 cup	cubed peeled pear (about 1)	250 mL
1 tbsp	olive oil	15 mL
1 tsp	crumbled dried rosemary (optional)	5 mL
½ cup	water (approx.)	125 mL

1. In a medium bowl, toss squash and pear with oil and rosemary, if using.

2. Arrange in a single layer on prepared baking sheet and roast in preheated oven until squash and pears are golden and tender, about 20 minutes. Let cool.

3. Transfer to blender, add water and purée on high speed, adding more water if necessary, until smooth.

Nutritional Information
(Per ¼-cup/50 mL Serving)

Calories	39 Kcal
Total Carbohydrates	6 g
Fiber	1 g
Fat	2 g
Protein	0 g
Iron	0 mg

Squash, Celery Root and Apples

1 cup	diced peeled acorn squash	250 mL
1 cup	diced peeled apple (about 1)	250 mL
½ cup	diced peeled celery root	125 mL
½ cup	unsweetened apple juice	125 mL
¼ tsp	ground nutmeg	1 mL

1. In a medium saucepan, over medium-low heat, combine squash, apple, celery root, apple juice and nutmeg. Bring to a simmer, cover and cook, stirring occasionally, until squash, celery root and apples are very tender, about 35 minutes. Let cool.

2. Transfer to blender and purée on high speed until smooth.

Nutritional Information
(Per ¼-cup/50 mL Serving)

Calories	24 Kcal
Total Carbohydrates	6 g
Fiber	1 g
Fat	0 g
Protein	0 g
Iron	0 mg

MAKES ABOUT 2 CUPS (500 ML)

Celeriac, or celery root, is the root of a specific variety of celery. Peel the tough outer skin before dicing the flesh inside.

VARIATION

Substitute an equal amount of chopped celery for the celery root.

*In general, the darker
the color of vegetable;
the stronger the taste.
If you don't succeed
with broccoli on its
own, try combining it
with any of your baby's
favorites until they
become used to it.*

Yummy Broccoli

| 3 cups | broccoli florets | 750 mL |
| 1/2 cup | unsweetened apple juice or water | 125 mL |

1. Place broccoli in a steaming basket fitted over a saucepan of boiling water. Cover and steam until broccoli is very tender, about 15 to 20 minutes. Let cool.

2. Transfer broccoli to blender, add apple juice and purée on high speed until smooth.

**Nutritional Information
(Per 1/4-cup/50 mL Serving)**

Calories. . . . . 22 Kcal
Total Carbohydrates . . . . 5 g
Fiber . . . . 1 g
Fat . . . . 0 g
Protein . . . . 1 g
Iron . . . . 0 mg
Vitamin C . . . . 25 mg

Celery Root, Carrots and Parsnips

1 cup	cubed peeled carrots (about 2)	250 mL
½ cup	cubed peeled celery root	125 mL
½ cup	cubed peeled parsnip (about 1)	125 mL

1. In a medium saucepan, over medium-high heat, combine carrots, celery root and parsnip. Pour in enough water just to cover. Bring to a boil. Cover, reduce heat and simmer until all vegetable are very tender, about 15 minutes. Let cool.

2. Transfer to blender with cooking liquid and purée on high speed until smooth.

**Nutritional Information
(Per ¼-cup/50 mL Serving)**

Calories	14 Kcal
Total Carbohydrates	3 g
Fiber	1 g
Fat	0 g
Protein	0 g
Iron	0 mg

**MAKES ABOUT
2 CUPS (500 ML)**

Sweet and mild root vegetables team up in this tasty purée!

TIP

Choose parsnips that are small and firm; larger, older parsnips have a higher starch content that may produce a purée that is too sticky once blended.

VARIATION

Substitute an equal amount of chopped celery for the celery root.

*Taste the fall harvest
in this rich vegetable
purée!*

Squashed Green Beans

1 cup	diced peeled butternut squash	250 mL
½ cup	unsweetened apple juice or water	125 mL
1½ cups	sliced trimmed green beans (about 6 oz/175 g)	375 mL

1. In a medium saucepan, over medium-high heat, combine squash and apple juice. Add enough water to completely cover squash. Cover and bring to a boil; reduce heat and simmer for 10 minutes. Add green beans, cover and cook until beans and squash are very tender, about 10 minutes. Let cool.

2. Transfer to blender with cooking liquid and purée on high speed until smooth.

**Nutritional Information
(Per ¼-cup/50 mL Serving)**

Calories	43 Kcal
Total Carbohydrates	11 g
Fiber	2 g
Fat	0 g
Protein	1 g
Iron	1 mg

Corny Sweet Potatoes

1½ cups	diced peeled sweet potato (about 1)	500 mL
1 cup	corn kernels	250 mL
¼ cup	orange juice	50 mL
1 tbsp	blackstrap molasses	15 mL

1. Place sweet potato in a steaming basket fitted over a saucepan of boiling water. Cover and steam until very tender, about 20 minutes. Add corn and steam for 2 minutes longer. Let cool.

2. Transfer sweet potato and corn to blender and add orange juice and molasses; purée on high speed until smooth.

**MAKES ABOUT
2 CUPS (500 ML)**

Molasses adds iron and a hint of sweetness to two favorites.

TIPS

There are many types of molasses available, but blackstrap has the least amount of sugar and the most nutrients.

Sweet potatoes are a good source of beta carotene.

**Nutritional Information
(Per ¼-cup/50 mL Serving)**

Calories	53 Kcal
Total Carbohydrates	12 g
Fiber	1 g
Fat	0 g
Protein	1 g
Iron	0 mg

**MAKES ABOUT
2 CUPS (500 ML)**

*Pairing broccoli with
the mild, sweet flavors
of squash and carrots
is a great way to
introduce it.*

TIPS

Cut the vegetables into
equal-sized pieces for
even cooking.

Cook vegetables until
they break apart when
pierced with a fork;
this will ensure the
smoothest consistency
when the vegetables
are puréed.

Squashed Vegetable Purée

1 cup	diced peeled butternut squash	250 mL
½ cup	sliced peeled broccoli stems	125 mL
½ cup	diced peeled carrot (about 1)	125 mL
¼ cup	orange juice	50 mL

1. Place squash, broccoli stems and carrot in a steaming basket fitted over a saucepan of boiling water. Cover and steam for 15 to 20 minutes, or until very tender. Let cool.

2. Transfer vegetables to blender, add orange juice and purée on high speed until smooth.

**Nutritional Information
(Per ¼-cup/50 mL Serving)**

Calories . . . . 16 Kcal
Total Carbohydrates . . . . 4 g
Fiber . . . . 1 g
Fat . . . .
Protein . . . .
Iron . . . . 0 mg

Summer Savory

1 tbsp	vegetable oil	15 mL
½ cup	sliced leeks, white and light green parts only	125 mL
1 cup	diced peeled potatoes (about 1 large)	250 mL
½ cup	frozen corn kernels	125 mL
½ cup	diced tomatoes	125 mL
½ cup	low-sodium vegetable stock	125 mL
1 tbsp	chopped fresh parsley	15 mL

1. In a medium saucepan, heat oil over medium-high heat. Add leeks and cook, stirring, until tender, but not browned, about 5 minutes.

2. Add potatoes, corn and tomatoes and cook, stirring, until potatoes are golden, about 5 minutes.

3. Add vegetable stock and reduce heat to medium. Cover and simmer until potatoes are tender, about 15 minutes. Stir in parsley. Let cool.

4. Transfer to blender with cooking liquid and purée on high speed until desired consistency is reached.

Nutritional Information (Per ¼-cup/50 mL Serving)	
Calories	47 Kcal
Total Carbohydrates	7 g
Fiber	1 g
Fat	2 g
Protein	2 g
Iron	0 mg

MAKES ABOUT 2 CUPS (500 ML)

Leeks have a delicate, subtle flavor that is much sweeter and milder than cooking onions. They're a great way to get your little one started.

VARIATION

Whisk ½ cup (125 mL) cold milk into 1 cup (250 mL) purée for a refreshing summer soup.

FOR OLDER KIDS

Serve as a dip with baked whole wheat tortilla or pita wedges.

Guacamole for Beginners

1 cup	sliced peeled avocado (about 1)	250 mL
½ cup	chopped peeled and seeded tomato	125 mL
2 tbsp	freshly squeezed lime juice	25 mL

1. In blender, combine avocado, tomato and lime juice and purée on high speed until smooth.

2. *Make ahead:* Store in an airtight container in the refrigerator for up to 3 days. Do not freeze.

**Nutritional Information
(Per ¼-cup/50 mL Serving)**

Calories	65 Kcal
Total Carbohydrates	4 g
Fiber	1 g
Fat	6 g
Protein	1 g
Iron	0 mg

FOOD FOR BABIES

Seven Months and Older

Meal Plans

Continue breastfeeding or formula feeding on demand while you are introducing infant cereals, vegetables, fruits and grains. Breast milk or formula is your child's best source of protein, fat and many vitamins and minerals, such as calcium. At this point, solid foods should be in addition to your regular breast milk or formula feedings. See the introduction for more information on these meal plans.

MEAL	1	2	3
Breakfast	• 2 tbsp (25 mL) prepared iron-fortified infant cereal • ¼ cup (50 mL) Banana (page 28)	• ¼ cup (50 mL) Peach and Banana Oatmeal (page 89) • ¼ cup (50 mL) Pears (page 36)	• 2 tbsp (25 mL) prepared iron-fortified infant cereal • ¼ cup (50 mL) Peach-Pear Bananarama (page 59)
Snack	• Breast or formula feeding on demand	• Breast or formula feeding on demand	• Breast or formula feeding on demand
Lunch	• ¼ cup (50 mL) Squash (page 52)	• ¼ cup (50 mL) Carrots (page 44)	• ¼ cup (50 mL) Avocado, Mango and Lime (page 67)
Snack	• Breast or formula feeding on demand	• Breast or formula feeding on demand	• Breast or formula feeding on demand
Supper	• ¼ cup (50 mL) Vegetable Paella (page 93) • ¼ cup (50 mL) Mango (page 32)	• ¼ cup (50 mL) Squash and Pepper Risotto (page 88) • ¼ cup (50 mL) Apples (page 26)	• ¼ cup (50 mL) Citrus Couscous (page 92) • ¼ cup (50 mL) Cherries (page 30)
Snack	• Breast or formula feeding on demand	• Breast or formula feeding on demand	• Breast or formula feeding on demand

Green Rice

2 tbsp	olive oil	25 mL
¼ cup	sliced onion	50 mL
1	clove garlic, minced	1
4 cups	leafy greens (spinach, Swiss chard or kale)	1 L
¼ tsp	salt	1 mL
¼ tsp	grated lemon zest	2 mL
1 cup	cooked rice, any variety	250 mL

MAKES ABOUT 2 CUPS (500 ML)

FOR OLDER KIDS

For more flavor, purée ¼ cup (50 mL) toasted pine nuts with the greens.

1. In a skillet, heat oil over medium-high heat. Add onion and cook, stirring occasionally, until tender, about 5 minutes. Add garlic and cook for 1 minute. Stir in greens until wilted, about 1 minute. Sprinkle with salt and lemon zest. Let cool slightly.

2. Transfer to blender and purée on high speed until smooth. Stir in rice until rice is coated with greens.

Nutritional Information
(Per ¼-cup/50 mL Serving)

Calories	65 Kcal
Total Carbohydrates	7 g
Fiber	1 g
Fat	3 g
Protein	1 g
Iron	Trace

Babies like cabbage's mild flavor, and it stimulates the appetite and has antidiarrheal and antibiotic properties. It also stimulates flatulence, so feed it to your baby in moderation.

TIP

If your baby is over eight months, serve with puréed pork or beef for a full meal.

VARIATION

Once your baby is used to cabbage, try the Savoy variety, which offers more flavor.

Brown Rice and Tomatoes with Cabbage

1 tbsp	vegetable oil	15 mL
1/2 cup	chopped onion	125 mL
1 cup	shredded cabbage	250 mL
1 1/4 cup	canned diced tomatoes, with juice	300 mL
1/2 cup	brown rice	125 mL
1/2 cup	water	125 mL

1. In a medium saucepan, heat oil over medium high heat. Add onion and cook, stirring, until tender, about 3 minutes. Add cabbage and cook, stirring occasionally, until softened, about 5 minutes.

2. Add tomatoes with juice, rice and water; bring to a boil. Cover, reduce heat and simmer until rice is tender and most of the liquid has been absorbed, about 40 minutes. Remove from heat and let stand, covered, for 5 minutes.

3. Transfer to blender and purée on high speed to desired consistency.

**Nutritional Information
(Per 1/4-cup/50 mL Serving)**

Calories	71 Kcal
Total Carbohydrates	12 g
Fiber	1 g
Fat	2 g
Protein	1 g
Iron	0 mg

Lentil and Rice Pilaf

1 tbsp	olive oil	15 mL
½ cup	chopped onion	125 mL
½ cup	long-grain white rice	125 mL
½ tsp	curry powder	2 mL
1 cup	low-sodium chicken stock	250 mL
1 cup	water	250 mL
½ cup	dried red lentils, rinsed	125 mL

1. In a medium saucepan, heat oil over medium-high heat. Add onion and cook, stirring, until tender, about 5 minutes. Stir in rice and curry powder until coated with oil. Pour in chicken stock, water and lentils; bring to a boil. Cover, reduce heat to low and simmer until liquid has been absorbed and rice and lentils are tender, about 20 minutes. Let cool.

2. Transfer to blender and purée on high speed to desired consistency.

MAKES ABOUT 2 CUPS (500 ML)

Lentils and rice work well in combination because they have complementary amino acids, enhancing the nutritional value of both foods.

TIP

Always rinse dried lentils well before using — they often contain small stones.

Nutritional Information (Per ¼-cup/50 mL Serving)	
Calories	108 Kcal
Total Carbohydrates	17 g
Fiber	4 g
Fat	2 g
Protein	6 g
Iron	2 mg

**MAKES ABOUT
2 CUPS (500 ML)**

*You are never too
young to love risotto!*

TIP

If your baby is over
eight months, serve
with chicken purée
for a complete meal.

Squash and Pepper Risotto

2 cups	low-sodium vegetable stock	500 mL
½ cup	Arborio or other short-grain rice	125 mL
½ cup	diced peeled butternut squash	125 mL
½ cup	chopped roasted red bell pepper	125 mL

1. In a medium saucepan, combine vegetable stock,
rice and squash; bring to a boil. Cover, reduce heat
and simmer, stirring occasionally, until rice is very
tender and most of the liquid has been absorbed,
about 20 minutes. Stir in red pepper.

2. Transfer to blender and purée on high speed to
desired consistency.

**Nutritional Information
(Per ¼-cup/50 mL Serving)**

Calories. . . . . 63 Kcal
Total Carbohydrates . . . . 12 g
Fiber . . . . 1 g
Fat . . . . 0 g
Protein . . . . 4 g
Iron . . . . 1 mg

Peach and Banana Oatmeal

1	banana, sliced	1
1 cup	cooked oatmeal	250 mL
1 cup	sliced, peeled peaches	250 mL

1. Place banana, oatmeal and peaches in blender; puréc on high speed until smooth.

**MAKES ABOUT
2 CUPS (500 ML)**

The carbohydrates provided by this hearty breakfast will give your little one lots of energy to get through the day.

Nutritional Information (Per ¼-cup/50 mL Serving)	
Calories	40 Kcal
Total Carbohydrates	9 g
Fiber	1 g
Fat	0 g
Protein	1 g
Iron	1 mg

*Millet cooks fairly
quickly, producing a
dish that is similar to
couscous but has its
own distinct flavor.*

Apricots with Ancient Grains

2 cups	water	500 mL
½ cup	millet	125 mL
1 cup	sliced fresh apricots	250 mL

1. In a small saucepan, over medium-high heat, bring water and millet just to a boil. Cover, reduce heat to low and simmer gently until millet is tender, about 30 minutes. Let stand, covered, until cooled slightly, about 15 minutes.

2. Transfer to blender, add apricots and purée on high speed until smooth.

**Nutritional Information
(Per ¼-cup/50 mL Serving)**

Calories	56 Kcal
Total Carbohydrates	11 g
Fiber	1 g
Fat	1 g
Protein	2 g
Iron	Trace

Quick and Easy Quinoa

1 cup	quinoa	250 mL
2 cups	vegetable stock or water	500 mL
¼ cup	grated Parmesan cheese	50 mL

1. In a large skillet, over medium-high heat, toast quinoa, shaking constantly, until golden, about 3 minutes. Add stock and bring to a boil. Reduce heat to low and simmer, uncovered, for 12 to 15 minutes, or until liquid has been absorbed. Let cool slightly.

2. Transfer to blender, add cheese and purée on high speed until combined.

Quinoa (pronounced "keen-wa") is a practical grain because it is easy to cook and is high in protein and minerals. Toasting it first gives it the best flavor.

**Nutritional Information
(Per ¼-cup/50 mL Serving)**

Calories	103 Kcal
Total Carbohydrates	15 g
Fiber	2 g
Fat	2 g
Protein	7 g
Iron	2 mg

**MAKES ABOUT
2 CUPS (500 ML)**

*Couscous refers to tiny
beads of semolina that
have been mixed with
cold salted water. It is
eaten much like rice
or other cereal grains.
This recipe calls for the
whole-wheat variety,
which has a slightly
nutty flavor.*

Citrus Couscous

½ cup	orange juice	125 mL
1 cup	low-sodium chicken stock	250 mL
1 cup	whole wheat couscous	250 mL
1 tbsp	olive oil	15 mL
¼ cup	chopped onion	50 mL
½ cup	chopped oranges	125 mL
1 tbsp	chopped parsley	15 mL

1. In a medium saucepan, bring orange juice and chicken stock to a boil. Add couscous; cover and remove from heat. Let sit for 5 minutes or until most of the liquid is absorbed and couscous is tender. Let cool.

2. Meanwhile, in a skillet, heat oil over medium-high heat. Add onion and cook, stirring, until tender, about 5 minutes.

3. Transfer onions and couscous to blender. Add oranges and purée on high speed to desired consistency. Sprinkle with parsley.

**Nutritional Information
(Per ¼-cup/50 mL Serving)**

Calories	117 Kcal
Total Carbohydrates	20 g
Fiber	1 g
Fat	2 g
Protein	4 g
Iron	Trace

Vegetable Paella

1 1/2 cups	low-sodium vegetable stock	375 mL
1/2 tsp	ground turmeric	2 mL
1 tbsp	olive oil	15 mL
1/4 cup	chopped onion	50 mL
1/2 cup	medium-grain rice, rinsed	125 mL
1/4 cup	chopped green bell pepper	50 mL
1/4 cup	chopped red bell pepper	50 mL
1/4 cup	frozen peas	50 mL

1. In a measuring cup, whisk together vegetable stock and turmeric.

2. In a skillet, heat oil over medium-high heat. Add onion and cook, stirring, until tender, about 3 minutes. Stir in rice, green pepper, red pepper, peas and stock mixture; bring to a boil. Reduce heat and simmer, partially covered, until rice is tender and liquid is absorbed, about 15 minutes.

3. Transfer to blender and purée on high speed to desired consistency.

Nutritional Information
(Per 1/4-cup/50 mL Serving)

Calories	74 Kcal
Total Carbohydrates	11 g
Fiber	1 g
Fat	2 g
Protein	3 g
Iron	1 mg
Vitamin C	15 mg

**MAKES ABOUT
2 CUPS (500 ML)**

This version of the traditional Spanish dish is quick and simple.

TIP

Combining vitamin C–rich foods with iron-rich foods helps the body absorb more iron. Red peppers are rich in vitamin C, and enriched rice is a good source of iron.

*Rice cooked in stock
with vegetables and
spice provides energy
for the day!*

TIP

For a flavor boost, add
a pinch of chili powder
to the carrot mixture.

Jumpin' Jambalaya

1 tbsp	olive oil	15 mL
½ cup	chopped peeled carrot	125 mL
¼ cup	chopped onion	50 mL
¼ cup	chopped celery	50 mL
¼ cup	long-grain white rice	50 mL
1 cup	low-sodium chicken stock	250 mL
1	bay leaf	1

1. In a skillet, heat oil over medium-high heat. Add carrot, onion and celery; cook, stirring, until onion is tender, about 5 minutes. Stir in rice until coated with oil. Add chicken stock and bay leaf; bring to a boil. Cover, reduce heat to low and simmer until rice is tender and most of the liquid has been absorbed, about 20 minutes. Let cool. Discard bay leaf.

2. Transfer to blender and purée on high speed to desired consistency.

**Nutritional Information
(Per ¼-cup/50 mL Serving)**

Calories	48 Kcal
Total Carbohydrates	6 g
Fiber	0 g
Fat	2 g
Protein	2 g
Iron	0 mg

FOOD FOR BABIES
Eight Months and Older

Continued on next page…

Meal Plans

At this age, babies are ready to try using a cup. Breast milk, formula and water are good choices to offer in a regular cup or a "sippy" cup. Continue breastfeeding or formula feeding on demand throughout the day. See the introduction for more information on these meal plans.

MEAL	1	2	3
Breakfast	• ½ cup (125 mL) prepared iron-fortified infant cereal • ¼ cup (50 mL) Cherried Peaches (page 59)	• ½ cup (125 mL) prepared iron-fortified infant cereal • ¼ cup (50 mL) Nectarines (page 34)	• ½ cup (125 mL) Peach and Banana Oatmeal (page 89) • Grapes, cut into 4 slices
Snack	• ½ slice whole wheat toast, dry • ¼ cup (50 mL) Strawberries (page 39) • Water	• Baby cookie • Diced canned peaches • Water	• ¼ cup (50 mL) puffed wheat cereal, dry • ¼ cup (50 mL) Watermelon Refresher (page 63) • Water
Lunch	• ¼ cup (50 mL) Pumpkin and Chickpea Stew (page 101)	• ¼ cup (50 mL) Carrots with Apricots and Berries (page 70)	• ¼ cup (50 mL) Chicken with Brown Rice and Peas (page 117)
Snack	• ¼ cup (50 mL) toasted oat cereal, dry • ¼ cup (50 mL) Apples (page 26)	• ¼ cup (50 mL) toasted oat cereal, dry • ¼ cup (50 mL) Strawberry Decadence (page 65)	• Baby cookie • ¼ cup (50 mL) Pumpkin and Apples (page 73)
Supper	• ¼ cup (50 mL) Pork with Apples and Cabbage (page 130) • Diced ripe pears • Water	• ¼ cup (50 mL) Haddock, Corn and Leeks (page 107) • ¼ cup (50 mL) Pears, Carrots and Squash (page 71) • Water	• ¼ cup (50 mL) Barley, Lentils and Sweet Potato (page 99) • Diced ripe banana • Water
Snack	• Breast or formula feeding on demand	• Breast or formula feeding on demand	• Breast or formula feeding on demand

*Lentils are an excellent
source of folic acid
and potassium. Adding
lentils to boiling liquid
makes them easier for
the baby to digest.
Mixed with rice, this
makes a complete meal.*

TIP

Lentils do not have to
be soaked, but rinse
well in a sieve and pick
through to remove any
small stones.

VARIATION

Substitute an equal
amount of red lentils
for the green lentils
and decrease the
cooking time in
Step 2 to 10 minutes.

Lentils, Carrots and Celery

1 tbsp	vegetable oil	15 mL
1/2 cup	chopped onion	125 mL
1/2 cup	chopped carrot	125 mL
1/2 cup	chopped celery	125 mL
2 cups	low-sodium vegetable stock	500 mL
1 cup	dried green lentils, rinsed	250 mL

1. In a medium saucepan, heat oil over medium-high heat. Add onion, carrot and celery and cook, stirring occasionally, until tender but not browned, about 5 minutes.

2. Add stock and lentils; cover, reduce heat and simmer until lentils are tender, about 30 minutes. Let cool.

3. Transfer to blender and purée on high speed until smooth.

**Nutritional Information
(Per 1/2-cup/125 mL Serving)**

Calories. . . . . 117 Kcal
Total Carbohydrates . . . . 16 g
Fiber . . . . 9 g
Fat . . . . 2 g
Protein . . . . 10 g
Iron . . . . 3 mg

Barley, Lentils and Sweet Potato

2 tsp	olive oil	10 mL
1	carrot, peeled and diced	1
1	stalk celery, diced	1
½	onion, diced	½
2 cups	low-sodium chicken stock	500 mL
½ cup	pearl barley, rinsed	125 mL
1 cup	diced peeled sweet potato	250 mL
¼ cup	dried green lentils, rinsed	50 mL

1. In a medium saucepan, heat oil over medium-high heat. Add carrot, celery and onion and cook, stirring occasionally, until carrots are tender, about 5 minutes.

2. Add stock and barley and bring to a boil. Cover, reduce heat and simmer for 20 minutes. Add sweet potato and lentils. Simmer until barley, lentils and sweet potato are very tender, about 25 minutes. Let cool.

3. Transfer to blender and purée on high speed until smooth.

MAKES ABOUT 3 CUPS (750 ML)

TIP

Add more chicken stock to this purée to make a great soup for the whole family.

**Nutritional Information
(Per ½-cup/125 mL Serving)**

Calories	148 Kcal
Total Carbohydrates	26 g
Fiber	6 g
Fat	2 g
Protein	8 g
Iron	2 mg

*Many of my students
would like to offer
beans and legumes to
their babies but aren't
sure what to do with
them — here's a simple
way to start.*

TIPS

Soaking dried beans
and legumes overnight
decreases cooking time,
preserves nutrients and
reduces the flatulence
they can cause.

Quick soak method:
In a saucepan, combine
3 parts water with 1 part
dried beans; bring to a
boil over medium heat.
Remove from heat and
let stand, covered, for
1 to 2 hours. Drain.
Cook according to
recipe.

Lemon Chickpeas with Carrots and Celery

1 cup	dried chickpeas	250 mL
2 cups	water	500 mL
1 tsp	vegetable oil	5 mL
¼ cup	diced onion	50 mL
¼ cup	diced celery	50 mL
¼ cup	diced peeled carrot	50 mL
1 cup	low-sodium vegetable stock	250 mL
1	bay leaf	1
1 tbsp	freshly squeezed lemon juice	15 mL
1 tbsp	chopped fresh parsley	15 mL

1. In a medium bowl, soak chickpeas in water overnight or for up to 1 day. Drain and set aside.

2. In a medium saucepan, heat oil over medium-high heat. Add onion, celery and carrot and cook until tender, about 5 minutes. Add stock, chickpeas and bay leaf; bring to a boil. Cover, reduce heat and simmer until chickpeas are very tender, about 45 minutes. Let cool.

3. Transfer to blender, add lemon juice and parsley and purée on high speed, adding water if necessary, until smooth.

**Nutritional Information
(Per ½-cup/125 mL Serving)**

Calories. . . . . 139 Kcal
Total Carbohydrates. . . . . 23 g
Fiber . . . . 5 g
Fat . . . . 2 g
Protein . . . . 8 g
Iron . . . . 2 mg

Pumpkin and Chickpea Stew

MAKES ABOUT 2 CUPS (500 ML)

1 cup	cubed peeled pumpkin	250 mL
½ cup	canned chickpeas, rinsed and drained	125 mL
½ cup	canned diced tomatoes, with juice	125 mL
1 tsp	crumbled dried sage	5 mL

TIP

Toss this purée with whole wheat couscous to make a nutritious vegetarian meal for the whole family.

1. In a medium saucepan, combine pumpkin, chickpeas, tomatoes with juice and sage; bring to a simmer. Cover and simmer until pumpkin is tender, about 15 minutes. Let cool.

2. Transfer to blender and purée on high speed to desired consistency.

Nutritional Information
(Per ½-cup/125 mL Serving)

Calories . . . . 46 Kcal
Total Carbohydrates . . . . 9 g
Fiber . . . . 1 g
Fat . . . . 1 g
Protein . . . . 2 g
Iron . . . . 1 mg

Don't assume your child will have the same food dislikes you do. Most food preferences are learned. Lima beans offer a smooth, buttery texture that appeals to babies.

VARIATION

Substitute an equal amount of water for the stock.

Summer Succotash

1 tbsp	vegetable oil	15 mL
½ cup	chopped onion	125 mL
1 cup	frozen corn	250 mL
1 cup	frozen lima beans	250 mL
1 cup	diced tomatoes	·250 mL
½ cup	low-sodium vegetable stock	125 mL
1 tbsp	chopped fresh parsley	15 mL

1. In a skillet, heat oil over medium-high heat. Add onion and cook until tender but not browned, about 5 minutes. Add corn, lima beans, tomatoes, stock and parsley; bring to a boil. Cover, reduce heat and simmer, stirring occasionally, until lima beans are tender, about 15 minutes. Let cool.

2. Transfer to blender and purée on high speed until smooth.

**Nutritional Information
(Per ¼-cup/50 mL Serving)**

Calories . . . . 72 Kcal
Total Carbohydrates . . . . 11 g
Fiber . . . . 2 g
Fat . . . . 2 g
Protein . . . . 3 g
Iron . . . . 1 mg

Hummus for Beginners

1 cup	rinsed and drained canned chickpeas	250 mL
½ cup	water	125 mL

1. In blender, on high speed, purée chickpeas until smooth.

2. *Make ahead:* Store in an airtight container in the refrigerator for up to 3 days. Do not freeze.

Nutritional Information
(Per ¼-cup/50 mL Serving)

Calories	71 Kcal
Total Carbohydrates	14 g
Fiber	3 g
Fat	1 g
Protein	3 g
Iron	1 mg

MAKES 1 CUP (250 ML)

FOR OLDER KIDS

Serve as a dip for vegetables and strips of baked whole wheat pitas.

**MAKES ABOUT
2 CUPS (500 ML)**

*This intensely colored
purée is packed full of
delicious nutrients.*

FOR OLDER KIDS

Serve as a dip with
warm naan bread or
whole wheat pita
wedges.

Dhal for Beginners

1 1/2 cups	low-sodium vegetable stock	375 mL
1/4 cup	dried red lentils, rinsed	50 mL
1/2 tsp	ground coriander	2 mL
1/4 tsp	ground turmeric	1 mL
1	small potato, peeled and diced	1
1	carrot, peeled and diced	1
1/2 cup	cauliflower florets	125 mL

1. In a medium saucepan, combine stock, lentils, coriander and turmeric; bring to a boil. Cover, reduce heat and simmer for 15 minutes, until lentils are slightly tender.

2. Stir in potato, carrot and cauliflower; cover and simmer until vegetables and lentils are very tender, about 15 minutes. Let cool.

3. Transfer to blender and purée on high speed until smooth.

**Nutritional Information
(Per 1/4-cup/50 mL Serving)**

Calories...................................84 Kcal
Total Carbohydrates........................13 g
Fiber......................................6 g
Fat..0 g
Protein....................................8 g
Iron.......................................2 mg

Fish and Mushy Peas

1 cup	frozen sweet peas	250 mL
6 oz	skinless cod,* haddock or halibut fillet	175 g
½ cup	low-sodium vegetable stock	125 mL
1 tsp	freshly squeezed lemon juice	5 mL

* Nutritional information is for cod

1. Arrange peas in a medium saucepan. Place fish on top and pour stock over fish. Cover and cook over medium heat until fish flakes easily when tested with a fork, about 10 minutes. Let cool.

2. Transfer to blender, add lemon juice and purée on high speed to desired consistency.

Nutritional Information
(Per ½-cup/125 mL Serving)

Calories	69 Kcal
Total Carbohydrates	5 g
Fiber	2 g
Fat	0 g
Protein	11 g
Iron	1 mg

MAKES ABOUT 2 CUPS (500 ML)

Lean white fish has a very mild flavor and can be quickly prepared.

FOR OLDER KIDS

Spoon ½ cup (125 mL) purée onto a split baked potato and sprinkle with shredded cheese. Bake in preheated 350°F (180°C) oven until potato is warmed through and cheese is melted, about 15 minutes.

**MAKES ABOUT
2 CUPS (500 ML)**

Celery brings great flavor to this delicate dish.

Cod with Celery and Peppers

6 oz	skinless cod fillet	175 g
1	stalk celery, diced	1
1 cup	diced red bell pepper	250 mL
1 cup	water	250 mL
¼ cup	long-grain white rice	50 mL

1. In a medium saucepan, combine cod, celery, red pepper, water and rice; bring to a boil over medium-high heat. Cover, reduce heat and simmer until fish flakes easily when tested with a fork and rice is tender, about 15 minutes. Let cool.

2. Transfer to blender and purée on high speed to desired consistency.

**Nutritional Information
(Per ½-cup/125 mL Serving)**

Calories . . . . 90 Kcal
Total Carbohydrates . . . . 12 g
Fiber . . . . 1 g
Fat . . . . 0 g
Protein . . . . 9 g
Iron . . . . 1 mg
Vitamin C . . . . 72 mg

Haddock, Corn and Leeks

2 tsp	olive oil	10 mL
½ cup	chopped leek, white and light green parts only	125 mL
1 cup	frozen sweet corn	250 mL
6 oz	skinless haddock fillet	175 g
¼ cup	water	50 mL

1. In a nonstick skillet, heat oil over medium-high heat. Add leeks and cook, stirring, until tender but not browned, about 3 minutes. Add corn and cook for 2 minutes more. Arrange haddock on top of leek-corn mixture and pour in water; cover and cook until fish flakes easily when tested with a fork, about 8 minutes. Let cool.

2. Transfer to blender and purée on high speed to desired consistency.

Nutritional Information
(Per ½-cup/125 mL Serving)

Calories	100 Kcal
Total Carbohydrates	10 g
Fiber	1 g
Fat	3 g
Protein	9 g
Iron	1 mg

MAKES ABOUT 2 CUPS (500 ML)

The mild flavor of this purée is especially pleasing to young palates.

TIP

Cooking the leek and corn first gives them a mild, sweet flavor. If you're in a hurry, omit the oil and cook the leek, corn, fish and water in a covered pot over medium-high heat until leek is tender and fish flakes easily when tested with a fork, about 8 minutes. Purée on high speed to desired consistency.

**MAKES ABOUT
2 CUPS (500 ML)**

*Oily fish, such as
salmon, are an excellent
source of iron. Iron is
absorbed more easily
when combined with
vitamin C, which in
this recipe is provided
by the broccoli.*

Cheesy Salmon and Broccoli Dinner

1 cup	broccoli florets	250 mL
1	small potato, peeled and diced	1
8 oz	skinless salmon fillets	250 g
1/2 cup	homogenized (whole) milk	125 mL
1/4 cup	shredded Cheddar cheese	50 mL

1. Arrange potatoes and broccoli in a medium saucepan. Lay salmon fillets on top and pour milk over salmon; bring to a boil over medium-high heat. Cover, reduce heat and simmer for 15 to 20 minutes, or until vegetables are tender and fish flakes easily when tested with a fork. Let cool.

2. Transfer to blender, add cheese and purée on high speed to desired consistency.

**Nutritional Information
(Per 1/2-cup/125 mL Serving)**

Calories. . . . . .133 Kcal
Total Carbohydrates . . . . .6 g
Fiber . . . . .1 g
Fat . . . . .5 g
Protein . . . . .15 g
Iron . . . . .1 mg
Vitamin C. . . . . .21 mg

Spinach, Salmon and Rice

2 tsp	olive oil	10 mL
¼ cup	chopped onion	50 mL
½ cup	long-grain white rice	125 mL
1 cup	water (approx.)	250 mL
1 cup	chopped fresh spinach	250 mL
4 oz	skinless salmon fillet	125 g
1 tsp	freshly squeezed lemon juice	5 mL

1. In a medium saucepan, heat oil over medium-high heat. Add onion and cook, stirring, until tender but not browned, about 3 minutes.

2. Add rice and stir until coated with oil. Stir in water and bring to a boil. Cover, reduce heat, and simmer until most of the water has been absorbed and rice is slightly tender, about 15 minutes.

3. Arrange spinach and salmon on top of rice; cover and continue to cook until spinach is wilted and salmon flakes easily when tested with a fork, about 10 minutes. Let sit, covered, for 10 minutes.

4. Transfer to blender, add lemon juice and purée on high speed to desired consistency, adding more water if necessary.

Nutritional Information
(Per ½-cup/125 mL Serving)

Calories	143 Kcal
Total Carbohydrates	20 g
Fiber	1 g
Fat	3 g
Protein	8 g
Iron	1 mg

MAKES ABOUT 2 CUPS (500 ML)

VARIATION

For the ultimate in nutritional density, substitute an equal amount of blanched Swiss chard for the spinach.

**MAKES ABOUT
2 CUPS (500 ML)**

The sweet flavor of this delicate white fish is a great way to introduce fish to your little one's diet.

VARIATION

Substitute halibut, orange roughy or cod for the tilapia.

Tilapia, Celery and Tomatoes

1 tbsp	olive oil	15 mL
½ cup	thinly sliced celery	125 mL
½ cup	sliced green onions	125 mL
½ cup	diced tomato	125 mL
½ tsp	dried dillweed	2 mL
4 oz	skinless tilapia fillet	175 g
½ cup	water	125 mL

1. In a medium saucepan, heat oil over medium-high heat. Add celery, green onions and tomato; cook, stirring occasionally, until celery is tender, about 5 minutes. Add tilapia and water; cover and cook until fish flakes easily when tested with a fork, about 5 minutes. Let cool.

2. Transfer to blender and purée on high speed until smooth.

**Nutritional Information
(Per ½-cup/125 mL Serving)**

Calories . . . . 64 Kcal
Total Carbohydrates . . . . 3 g
Fiber . . . . 1 g
Fat . . . . 4 g
Protein . . . . 6 g
Iron . . . . 0 mg

Trout, Zucchini and Potatoes

1	medium Yukon golden potato, peeled and diced	1
1	zucchini, diced	1
6 oz	trout fillet	175 g
	Water	

**MAKES ABOUT
2 CUPS (500 ML)**

The mild flavor of zucchini blends well with tender pink trout.

TIP

The pink flesh of the trout gives this savory purée a beautiful color, but other fish can be substituted and cooked in the same manner.

1. Arrange potato and zucchini in a medium saucepan. Lay trout on top, skin side down, and add enough water to almost cover potato and zucchini; cover and bring to a boil over medium-high heat. Reduce heat and simmer until potatoes are tender and trout flakes easily when tested with a fork, about 15 minutes. Let cool.

2. Remove skin from trout. Transfer to blender with potato-zucchini mixture and cooking liquid; purée on high speed, adding more water if necessary, until smooth.

**Nutritional Information
(Per ½-cup/125 mL Serving)**

Calories	96 Kcal
Total Carbohydrates	7 g
Fiber	1 g
Fat	3 g
Protein	10 g
Iron	1 mg

TIPS

Roasted or poached chicken can be blended in the same manner.

For better flavor, substitute an equal amount of low-sodium chicken stock for the water.

Chicken

| 8 oz | boneless skinless chicken breast, cut in strips | 250 g |
| 1 cup | water | 250 mL |

1. Arrange chicken in a steamer basket fitted over a saucepan of boiling water. Cover and steam until chicken is no longer pink inside, about 20 minutes. Let cool.

2. Transfer to blender, add water and purée on high speed to desired consistency.

**Nutritional Information
(Per ¼-cup/50 mL Serving)**

Calories.................................50 Kcal
Total Carbohydrates...........................0 g
Fiber...0 g
Fat...1 g
Protein....................................10 g
Iron......................................1 mg

Chicken with Celery

6 oz	boneless skinless chicken breast, diced	175 g
1 cup	chopped celery	250 mL
1 cup	low-sodium chicken stock	250 mL

1. In a medium saucepan, combine chicken, celery and stock; bring to a simmer over medium heat. Cover and simmer until celery is very tender and chicken is no longer pink inside, about 15 minutes. Let cool.

2. Transfer to blender and purée on high speed until smooth.

**Nutritional Information
(Per ½-cup/125 mL Serving)**

Calories	42 Kcal
Total Carbohydrates	2 g
Fiber	1 g
Fat	0 g
Protein	8 g
Iron	1 mg

**MAKES ABOUT
2 CUPS (500 ML)**

Kids love the mild flavors of chicken and celery.

TIP

For a smooth purée, remove the tough fibers from the celery ribs before chopping.

FOR OLDER KIDS

Stir purée into cooked brown rice for a quick meal.

MAKES ABOUT
2 CUPS (500 ML)

Roasted red pepper adds smoky sweetness to chicken and corn.

Chicken with Red Pepper and Corn

1 tbsp	olive oil	15 mL
6 oz	boneless skinless chicken breast, chopped	175 g
¼ cup	chopped onion	50 mL
½ cup	chopped roasted red bell pepper	125 mL
½ cup	frozen sweet corn	125 mL
1 tbsp	chopped fresh parsley	15 mL
½ cup	low-sodium chicken stock	125 mL

1. In a skillet, heat oil over medium-high heat. Add chicken, turning to brown evenly; transfer to a plate.

2. Add onion to skillet and cook, stirring, until tender, about 5 minutes. Stir in pepper, corn and parsley; cook for 2 minutes. Add stock and bring to a boil. Add browned chicken; cover, reduce heat and simmer until chicken is no longer pink inside and sauce thickens slightly. Let cool.

3. Transfer to blender and purée on high speed to desired consistency.

**Nutritional Information
(Per ½-cup/125 mL Serving)**

Calories. . . . . 110 Kcal
Total Carbohydrates . . . . 6 g
Fiber . . . . 1 g
Fat . . . . 5 g
Protein . . . . 12 g
Iron . . . . 1 mg
Vitamin C . . . . 15 mg

Avocado with Chicken

8 oz	boneless skinless chicken breast, cut in strips	250 g
1	avocado, peeled, pitted and sliced	1
1 tbsp	freshly squeezed lime juice	15 mL
¾ cup	low-sodium chicken stock	175 mL

MAKES ABOUT 2 CUPS (500 ML)

TIP

Cooking time depends on the thickness of the chicken breast.

FOR OLDER KIDS

Serve as a dip with baked whole wheat tortilla wedges.

1. Arrange chicken in a steamer basket fitted over a saucepan of boiling water. Cover and steam for 10 to 15 minutes, until chicken is no longer pink inside. Transfer to a cutting board and cut into 1-inch (2.5 cm) pieces. Let cool.

2. Transfer to blender and add avocado, lime juice and stock; purée on high speed to desired consistency.

3. *Make ahead:* Store in an airtight container in the refrigerator for up to 3 days. Do not freeze.

**Nutritional Information
(Per ½-cup/125 mL Serving)**

Calories	119 Kcal
Total Carbohydrates	3 g
Fiber	1 g
Fat	7 g
Protein	12 g
Iron	1 mg

*This autumn harvest
dish is both sweet and
savory!*

VARIATION

Substitute turkey breast
for the chicken.

Chicken with Pumpkin

1 tbsp	olive oil	15 mL
6 oz	boneless skinless chicken breast, diced	175 g
1 cup	cubed peeled pie pumpkin	250 mL
½ cup	low-sodium chicken stock	125 mL
½ tsp	ground cinnamon	2 mL
¼ tsp	ground allspice	1 mL
¼ tsp	ground ginger	1 mL

1. In a medium saucepan, heat oil over medium heat. Add chicken, turning to brown evenly. Stir in pumpkin, stock, cinnamon, allspice and ginger; bring to a boil. Cover, reduce heat and simmer until chicken is no longer pink inside and pumpkin is very tender, about 20 minutes. Let cool.

2. Transfer to blender and purée on high speed until smooth.

**Nutritional Information
(Per ½-cup/125 mL Serving)**

Calories . . . . 70 Kcal
Total Carbohydrates . . . . 3 g
Fiber . . . . 0 g
Fat . . . . 4 g
Protein . . . . 7 g
Iron . . . . 1 mg

Chicken with Brown Rice and Peas

1 tbsp	olive oil	15 mL
6 oz	boneless skinless chicken thighs, chopped	175 g
½ cup	chopped onion	125 mL
½ tsp	curry powder	2 mL
1 ½ cups	low-sodium chicken stock	375 mL
½ cup	long-grain brown rice, rinsed	125 mL
1 cup	frozen sweet peas	250 mL

MAKES ABOUT 2 CUPS (500 ML)

A small amount of curry powder provides taste without heat, and will give little ones a palate for flavor!

TIP

Use whole-grain products such as brown rice and whole wheat bread to increase daily fiber intake

1. In a medium saucepan, heat oil over medium-high heat. Add chicken, turning to brown evenly; transfer to a plate.

2. Add onion and curry powder to saucepan; cook, stirring, until onion is tender but not browned, about 3 minutes. Stir in stock and rice; bring to a boil. Cover, reduce heat and simmer for 25 to 30 minutes, or until rice is almost tender. Add peas and browned chicken; simmer until chicken is no longer pink inside, about 10 minutes. Let cool.

3. Transfer to blender and purée on high speed to desired consistency.

Nutritional Information
(Per ½-cup/125 mL Serving)

Calories	193 Kcal
Total Carbohydrates	26 g
Fiber	3 g
Fat	5 g
Protein	11 g
Iron	2 mg

**MAKES ABOUT
2 CUPS (500 ML)**

*Couscous is a quick,
simple grain to prepare.
Choose the whole-wheat
variety to maximize
flavor and nutrition.*

Chicken and Citrus Couscous

½ cup	orange juice	125 mL
1 cup	low-sodium chicken stock	250 mL
1 cup	whole wheat couscous	250 mL
1 tbsp	olive oil	15 mL
6 oz	boneless skinless chicken breast, chopped	175 g
¼ cup	chopped onion	50 mL
1 tbsp	chopped parsley	15 mL

1. In a medium saucepan, bring orange juice and chicken stock to a boil. Add couscous; cover and remove from heat. Let sit for 5 minutes or until most of the liquid is absorbed and couscous is tender. Let cool.

2. Meanwhile, in a skillet, heat oil over medium-high heat. Add chicken, turning, until evenly browned and no longer pink inside, about 5 minutes; transfer to a plate. Let cool. Add onion to skillet; cook, stirring, until tender, about 5 minutes.

3. Transfer onions, chicken and couscous to blender and purée on high speed to desired consistency. Sprinkle with parsley.

**Nutritional Information
(Per ½-cup/125 mL Serving)**

Calories	261 Kcal
Total Carbohydrates	38 g
Fiber	2 g
Fat	4 g
Protein	16 g
Iron	1 mg

Chicken Divine

1 tbsp	vegetable oil	15 mL
6 oz	boneless skinless chicken breast or thighs, chopped	175 g
½ cup	chopped onion	125 mL
½ cup	sliced white mushrooms	125 mL
1 cup	fresh broccoli florets	250 mL
¼ cup	shredded Cheddar cheese	50 mL

1. In a nonstick skillet, heat oil over medium-high heat. Add chicken, turning to brown evenly; transfer to a plate.

2. Add onion to skillet and cook, stirring, until tender, about 5 minutes. Add mushrooms and cook, stirring, until golden, about 7 minutes. Add water, broccoli and browned chicken; bring just to a boil. Cover, reduce heat and simmer until broccoli is very tender and chicken is no longer pink inside, about 10 minutes. Let cool.

3. Transfer to blender, sprinkle with cheese and purée on high speed to desired consistency.

MAKES ABOUT 2 CUPS (500 ML)

This flavor combination is a favorite no matter what your age!

TIP

If you prefer, you can use frozen broccoli instead of fresh. Place frozen broccoli in a strainer and run it under hot water for 30 seconds, then drain well before using. (That way, it won't add too much extra water.)

Nutritional Information (Per ½-cup/125 mL Serving)	
Calories	132 Kcal
Total Carbohydrates	3 g
Fiber	1 g
Fat	9 g
Protein	10 g
Iron	1 mg
Vitamin C	18 mg

8

Ripe mango provides vitamins A and C and gives a mild, sweet flavor to this protein-rich dish. Mango skin can irritate a baby's mouth, so always peel before using.

TIP

Mangoes with shriveled skin tend to have fibrous flesh that is very acidic and unpleasant-tasting. Ripe mangoes have a sweet, fragrant aroma and yield slightly to the touch.

Tropical Chicken

1 tbsp	vegetable oil	15 mL
¼ cup	diced onion	50 mL
6 oz	boneless skinless chicken breast, chopped	175 g
¼ cup	long-grain brown rice, rinsed	50 mL
½ cup	low-sodium chicken stock	125 mL
½ cup	diced peeled mango	125 mL

1. In a medium saucepan, heat oil over medium-high heat. Add onion and cook, stirring, until tender but not browned, about 5 minutes. Add chicken and cook, stirring, until lightly browned, about 7 minutes. Stir in rice and cook for 1 minute more. Stir in stock and mango; bring to a boil. Cover, reduce heat and simmer until rice is tender and chicken is no longer pink inside, about 40 minutes. Let cool.

2. Transfer to blender and purée on high speed to desired consistency.

**Nutritional Information
(Per ½-cup/125 mL Serving)**

Calories	127 Kcal
Total Carbohydrates	13 g
Fiber	1 g
Fat	2 g
Protein	13 g
Iron	1 mg

Chicken Stew

1 tbsp	vegetable oil	15 mL
6 oz	boneless skinless chicken breast, chopped	175 g
½ cup	diced peeled carrot	125 mL
¼ cup	diced onion	50 mL
¼ cup	diced celery	50 mL
1	small potato, cubed	1
1 cup	low-sodium chicken stock	250 mL
1 tbsp	minced fresh parsley	15 mL

1. In a medium saucepan, heat oil over medium-high heat. Add chicken, turning to brown evenly; transfer to a plate.

2. Add carrot, onion and celery to saucepan; cook until tender but not browned, about 5 minutes. Stir in potato and stock; bring to a boil. Return browned chicken to pan. Cover, reduce heat and simmer until potatoes are very tender and chicken is no longer pink inside, about 20 minutes. Stir in parsley. Let cool.

3. Transfer to blender and purée on high speed to desired consistency.

Nutritional Information (Per ½-cup/125 mL Serving)	
Calories	120 Kcal
Total Carbohydrates	7 g
Fiber	1 g
Fat	4 g
Protein	14 g
Iron	1 mg

MAKES ABOUT 2 CUPS (500 ML)

Classic comfort food for your baby!

FOR OLDER KIDS

Put ½ cup (125 mL) purée in a ramekin or gratin dish. Use refrigerated dinner-roll dough (cut to fit) to cover, using excess to form your child's initial and place on top. Bake in preheated 350°F (180°C) oven until pastry is golden and filling is warm, about 12 minutes.

8

**MAKES ABOUT
2 CUPS (500 ML)**

*This purée has a great
balance of protein,
vegetables and
carbohydrates and
will help your child
get through an
action-packed day.*

TIP

For a flavor boost, add
a pinch of chili powder
to the carrot mixture.

Chicken Jambalaya

1 tbsp	olive oil	15 mL
6 oz	boneless skinless chicken breast, chopped	175 mL
½ cup	chopped peeled carrot	125 mL
¼ cup	chopped onion	50 mL
¼ cup	chopped celery	50 mL
¼ cup	long-grain white rice	50 mL
1 cup	low-sodium chicken stock	250 mL
1	bay leaf	1

1. In a skillet, heat oil over medium-high heat. Add chicken, turning to brown evenly; transfer to a plate. Add carrot, onion and celery to skillet. Cook, stirring, until onion is tender, about 5 minutes. Stir in rice until coated with oil. Add chicken stock and bay leaf. Bring to a boil and add chicken, with any accumulated juices, back to skillet. Cover, reduce heat to low and simmer until rice is tender and most of the liquid has been absorbed, about 20 minutes. Let cool. Discard bay leaf.

2. Transfer to blender and purée on high speed to desired consistency.

**Nutritional Information
(Per ½-cup/125 mL Serving)**

Calories. . . . . 134 Kcal
Total Carbohydrates . . . . 12 g
Fiber . . . . 1 g
Fat . . . . 4 g
Protein . . . . 12 g
Iron . . . . 1 mg

Turkey with Cranberries

1 tbsp	olive oil	15 mL
½ cup	diced peeled carrot	125 mL
½ cup	diced onion	125 mL
¼ cup	diced celery	50 mL
½ tsp	dried thyme	2 mL
6 oz	boneless skinless turkey breast, chopped	175 g
½ cup	low-sodium chicken stock	125 mL
¼ cup	fresh or frozen cranberries	50 mL

1. In a medium saucepan, heat oil over medium-high heat. Add carrot, onion, celery and thyme, stirring to combine. Cook, stirring, until vegetables are tender, about 5 minutes.

2. Add turkey and brown slightly. Stir in stock and cranberries, scraping any brown bits from bottom of pan; bring to a boil. Cover, reduce heat and simmer until cranberries are very tender and turkey is no longer pink inside, about 30 minutes. Let cool.

3. Transfer to blender and purée on high speed to desired consistency.

**Nutritional Information
(Per ½-cup/125 mL Serving)**

Calories	115 Kcal
Total Carbohydrates	5 g
Fiber	1 g
Fat	6 g
Protein	10 g
Iron	1 mg

**MAKES ABOUT
2 CUPS (500 ML)**

Don't leave your little one out over the holidays!

TIPS

Use 1 cup (250 mL) chopped leftover cooked turkey and add it just before puréeing.

For a simple risotto, stir into cooked rice with a little chicken stock.

**MAKES ABOUT
2 CUPS (500 ML)**

TIP

For better flavor,
substitute an equal
amount of low-sodium
beef stock for the
water.

Beef

| 8 oz | lean ground sirloin beef | 250 g |
| 1 cup | water | 250 mL |

1. In a skillet, brown beef over medium-high heat, breaking up any large pieces, until no longer pink, about 7 minutes. Drain and let cool.

2. Transfer to blender, add water and purée on high speed until smooth.

**Nutritional Information
(Per ¼-cup/50 mL Serving)**

Calories . . . . 115 Kcal
Total Carbohydrates . . . . 0 g
Fiber . . . . 0 g
Fat . . . . 8 g
Protein . . . . 10 g
Iron . . . . 1 mg

Beefy Broccoli

6 oz	lean ground sirloin beef	175 g
2 cups	chopped broccoli florets and stems	500 mL
½ cup	low-sodium beef stock	125 mL

1. In a skillet, brown beef over medium-high heat, breaking up any large pieces, until no longer pink, about 7 minutes. Drain off fat and return beef to skillet.

2. Add broccoli and stock; cover, reduce heat and simmer until broccoli is very tender, about 15 minutes. Let cool.

3. Transfer to blender and purée on high speed to desired consistency.

MAKES ABOUT 2 CUPS (500 ML)

FOR OLDER KIDS

Stir into cooked egg noodles for a simple weeknight meal.

Nutritional Information
(Per ½-cup/125 mL Serving)

Calories. . . . . 85 Kcal
Total Carbohydrates . . . . 3 g
Fiber . . . . 1 g
Fat . . . . 5 g
Protein . . . . 8 g
Iron . . . . 1 mg
Vitamin C . . . . 41 mg

*Carrots and orange
juice are the perfect
accompaniments
to beef.*

Beef with Carrots and Orange

6 oz	lean ground sirloin beef	175 g
1 cup	cubed peeled carrots (about 2)	250 mL
1 cup	unsweetened orange juice	250 mL

1. In a nonstick skillet, brown beef over medium-high heat, breaking up any large pieces, until no longer pink, about 7 minutes. Drain off fat and return beef to skillet.

2. Add carrots and orange juice, bring to a boil. Cover, reduce heat and simmer until carrots are very tender, about 20 minutes. Let cool.

3. Transfer to blender and purée on high speed to desired consistency.

**Nutritional Information
(Per 1/2-cup/125 mL Serving)**

Calories. . . . . 141 Kcal
Total Carbohydrates . . . . 10 g
Fiber . . . . 1 g
Fat . . . . 7 g
Protein . . . . 11 g
Iron . . . . 1 mg
Vitamin C . . . . 34 mg

Chili for Beginners

6 oz	lean ground sirloin beef	175 g
1 cup	canned diced tomatoes, with juice	250 mL
½ cup	rinsed and drained canned red kidney beans	125 mL
¼ cup	diced green bell pepper	50 mL
¼ cup	frozen corn	50 mL

1. In a skillet, brown beef over medium-high heat, breaking up any large pieces, until no longer pink, about 7 minutes. Drain off fat and return beef to skillet.

2. Add tomatoes with juice, kidney beans, green pepper and corn. Cover, reduce heat and simmer for 15 minutes, until vegetables are very tender. Let cool.

3. Transfer to blender and purée on high speed to desired consistency.

Nutritional Information (Per ½-cup/125 mL Serving)	
Calories	117 Kcal
Total Carbohydrates	10 g
Fiber	3 g
Fat	5 g
Protein	8 g
Iron	1 mg

MAKES ABOUT 2 CUPS (500 ML)

Start this family favorite from the beginning!

FOR OLDER KIDS

Spoon into a hollowed-out whole wheat dinner roll and sprinkle with shredded cheese. Bake in preheated 350°F (180°C) oven until cheese is melted, about 5 minutes.

Spoon ½ cup (125 mL) chili onto a split baked sweet potato and sprinkle with shredded Cheddar cheese. Bake in preheated 350°F (180°C) oven until cheese is melted and potato is warmed through, about 15 minutes. Top with sour cream and sliced green onions.

**MAKES ABOUT
2 CUPS (500 ML)**

*You're never too young
to fall in love with
comfort foods!*

VARIATION

Substitute ground pork
or chicken for the beef.

Shepherd's Pie

1	small Yukon gold potato, peeled and cubed	1
6 oz	lean ground sirloin beef	175 g
¼ cup	chopped onion	50 mL
¼ cup	chopped peeled carrot	50 mL
¼ cup	frozen peas	50 mL
¼ cup	frozen corn	50 mL

1. Place potato in a small saucepan of salted water and bring to a boil over medium-high heat; cook potato until tender, about 15 minutes. Drain.

2. Meanwhile, in a skillet, brown beef over medium-high heat, breaking up any large pieces, until no longer pink, about 7 minutes. Drain off fat and return to skillet. Add onion, carrot, peas and corn; cook, stirring occasionally, until onion and carrot are tender, about 10 minutes. Let cool.

3. Transfer to blender, add potato and purée on high speed to desired consistency.

**Nutritional Information
(Per ½-cup/125 mL Serving)**

Calories. . . . . 117 Kcal
Total Carbohydrate. . . . . 9 g
Fiber . . . . 2 g
Fat . . . . 6 g
Protein . . . . 7 g
Iron . . . . 1 mg

Pork

8 oz	pork tenderloin, diced	250 g
1 cup	water	250 mL

1. In a medium saucepan, over medium heat, bring pork and water just to a boil. Cover, reduce heat and simmer until pork is no longer pink inside, about 15 minutes. Let cool.

2. Transfer to blender and purée on high speed until smooth.

**Nutritional Information
(Per ¼-cup/50 mL Serving)**

Calories	68 Kcal
Total Carbohydrates	0 g
Fiber	0 g
Fat	2 g
Protein	12 g
Iron	1 mg

**MAKES ABOUT
2 CUPS (500 ML)**

Use lean cuts of pork that have not been salted or cured. Avoid bacon, sausages and deli meats — they have too much sodium and nitrates for little digestive systems.

Classic autumn flavors combine to make a savory dish sure to please baby's palate.

TIP

Golden Delicious apples are an ideal cooking apple because they retain their flavor when cooked.

Pork with Apples and Cabbage

1 tbsp	vegetable oil	15 mL
1/2 cup	diced onion	125 mL
8 oz	boneless pork loin chops, sliced	250 g
1	apple, peeled, cored and cubed	1
1 cup	shredded Savoy cabbage	250 mL
1/2 cup	sweetened apple juice or water (approx.)	125 mL

1. In a nonstick skillet, heat oil over medium-high heat. Add onion and cook, stirring, until tender but not browned, about 5 minutes. Add pork, turning to brown evenly. Add apple and cabbage; cook, stirring occasionally, for 5 minutes.

2. Pour apple juice into skillet; cover and cook, stirring occasionally, until cabbage and apple are very tender and pork is no longer pink inside, about 20 minutes. Let cool.

3. Transfer to blender and purée on high speed to desired consistency, adding more apple juice if necessary.

**Nutritional Information
(Per 1/2-cup/125 mL Serving)**

Calories	137 Kcal
Total Carbohydrates	10 g
Fiber	2 g
Fat	6 g
Protein	11 g
Iron	1 mg

Pork with Prunes and Apples

¼ cup	pitted prunes	50 mL
½ cup	sweetened apple juice	125 mL
2 tsp	olive oil	10 mL
6 oz	boneless pork loin chop, sliced	175 g
¼ cup	sliced onion	50 mL
1	apple, peeled, cored and sliced	1

1. In a small bowl, pour apple juice over prunes; let sit for 15 minutes, until slightly softened.

2. Meanwhile, in a skillet, heat oil over medium-high heat. Add pork, turning to brown evenly. Transfer to a plate.

3. Add onion to skillet and cook, stirring, until tender and golden, about 5 minutes. Add apple and cook, stirring, for 5 minutes more. Stir in prunes with juice and browned pork; cover, reduce heat and simmer until apple and prunes are very tender and pork is no longer pink inside, about 10 minutes. Let cool.

4. Transfer to blender and purée on high speed to desired consistency.

Nutritional Information
(Per ½-cup/125 mL Serving)

Calories	120 Kcal
Total Carbohydrates	16 g
Fiber	2 g
Fat	4 g
Protein	6 g
Iron	1 mg

MAKES ABOUT 2 CUPS (500 ML)

This purée is packed full of fruit and fiber to keep your little one "moving"!

TIP

If constipation is an issue, increase the prunes to ½ cup (125 mL) and omit the onions.

TIP

Add vegetable stock or more chicken stock to make a great soup for the whole family.

Ham and Split Peas

2 tsp	olive oil	10 mL
1	carrot, peeled and diced	1
1	celery stalk, diced	1
½	onion, diced	½
½ cup	diced cooked ham (about 4 oz/125 g)	125 mL
1 cup	low-sodium chicken stock	250 mL
½ cup	dried split yellow peas, rinsed	125 mL

1. In a medium saucepan, heat oil over medium-high heat. Add carrot, celery, onion and ham; cook, stirring occasionally, until carrots are tender, about 7 minutes.

2. Add stock and peas; cover, reduce heat and simmer until peas are tender, about 45 minutes. Let cool.

3. Transfer to blender and purée on high speed until smooth.

**Nutritional Information
(Per ½-cup/125 mL Serving)**

Calories. . . . . 160 Kcal
Total Carbohydrates. . . . . 19 g
Fiber . . . . 7 g
Fat . . . . 4 g
Protein . . . . 12 g
Iron . . . . 2 mg

Ham with Swiss Chard and Potatoes

1 tbsp	olive oil	15 mL
¼ cup	sliced onion	50 mL
½ cup	diced cooked ham (about 4 oz/125 g)	125 mL
1	small potato, peeled and cubed	1
2 cups	chopped Swiss chard	500 mL
½ cup	low-sodium vegetable stock (approx.)	125 mL

MAKES ABOUT 2 CUPS (500 ML)

This hearty winter purée will keep your little one satisfied all day!

1. In a medium saucepan, heat oil over medium-high heat. Add onion and cook, stirring, until tender but not browned, about 5 minutes. Add ham and cook, stirring, until lightly browned, about 3 minutes. Stir in potato, Swiss chard and stock. Cover, reduce heat and simmer until potato is tender, about 15 minutes. Let cool.

2. Transfer to blender and purée on high speed to desired consistency, adding more stock if necessary.

Nutritional Information
(Per ½-cup/125 mL Serving)

Calories	89 Kcal
Total Carbohydrates	6 g
Fiber	1 g
Fat	5 g
Protein	5 g
Iron	1 mg

Many little ones will reject meat, especially as they reach toddlerhood. Tofu provides a nutritious alternative and requires minimal effort to prepare. It has a mild, nutty flavor that can be disguised by anything it is cooked with — perfect for babies. Try it!

Tofu

| 1 cup | cubed firm tofu (about 4 oz/125 g) | 250 mL |

1. Place tofu in blender and purée on high speed until smooth.

Nutritional Information
(Per ¼-cup/50 mL Serving)

Calories	49 Kcal
Total Carbohydrates	2 g
Fiber	0 g
Fat	3 g
Protein	5 g
Iron	1 mg

Adding tofu to fruit makes a simple complete meal without any fuss.

FOR OLDER KIDS

This recipe, or any recipe that combines silken tofu and puréed fruits, can help toddlers who avoid meat get some protein.

Apples, Plums and Tofu

2	plums, peeled and pitted	2
1 cup	unsweetened applesauce	250 mL
¼ cup	silken tofu (about 2 oz/60 g)	50 mL

1. Combine plums, applesauce and tofu in blender and purée on high speed until smooth.

Nutritional Information
(Per ½-cup/125 mL Serving)

Calories	55 Kcal
Total Carbohydrates	11 g
Fiber	1 g
Fat	1 g
Protein	2 g
Iron	1 mg

Apricots, Pears and Tofu

4	ripe apricots, pits removed	4
1	ripe pear, peeled and sliced	1
¼ cup	silken tofu (about 2 oz/60 g)	50 mL

1. Combine apricots, pear and tofu in blender and purée on high speed until smooth.

Nutritional Information
(Per ½-cup/125 mL Serving)

Calories	39 Kcal
Total Carbohydrates	7 g
Fiber	1 g
Fat	1 g
Protein	2 g
Iron	1 mg

**MAKES ABOUT
2 CUPS (500 ML)**

Adding tofu to any of the vegetable or fruit recipes in previous sections will offer your baby protein without the fuss of cooking meat.

TIP

"Silken" refers to the texture of the tofu; it has a greater amount of liquid.

*This complete meal is
nutritious and has a
sweet, mellow flavor
that babies love.*

Butternut Squash, Corn and Tofu

1 cup	diced peeled butternut squash	250 mL
1 cup	low-sodium vegetable stock	250 mL
½ cup	frozen corn	125 mL
¼ cup	silken tofu (about 2 oz/60 g)	50 mL

1. In a medium saucepan, bring squash and stock to a boil over medium-high heat. Cover, reduce heat and simmer until squash is tender, about 20 minutes. Stir in corn and cook for 5 minutes more. Let cool.

2. Transfer to blender, add tofu and purée on high speed until smooth.

**Nutritional Information
(Per ½-cup/125 mL Serving)**

Calories . . . . 58 Kcal
Total Carbohydrates . . . . 9 g
Fiber . . . . 2 g
Fat . . . . 1 g
Protein . . . . 5 g
Iron . . . . 2 mg

FOOD FOR BABIES

Nine Months and Older

Meal Plans

At this age, your child can start to eat dairy foods such as yogurt and cheese, as well as adapted table food: diced fruits and cooked vegetables, tender chopped meats and casseroles with noodles cut up. Do not purée food until it is perfectly smooth — leave a few lumps to help your baby discover new textures. See the introduction for more information on these meal plans.

MEAL	1	2	3
Breakfast	• ½ cup (125 mL) prepared iron-fortified infant cereal • ¼ cup (50 mL) Avocado, Banana and Yogurt (page 144) • Breast or formula feeding	• ½ cup (125 mL) Fruity Breakfast Rice (page 147) • Breast or formula feeding	• ½ cup (125 mL) prepared iron-fortified infant cereal • ¼ cup (50 mL) Banana Cherry Blast (page 141) • Breast or formula feeding
Snack	• ¼ cup (50 mL) Fruit Custard (page 142) • ¼ tortilla spread with cream cheese • Water	• ¼ cup (50 mL) Mango (page 32) • Whole wheat toast with margarine • Water	• ¼ cup (50 mL) Blueberries (page 29) • ¼ cup (50 mL) puffed rice cereal, dry • Water
Lunch	• ½ cup (125 mL) Chicken Stew (page 121) • Breast or formula feeding	• ½ cup (125 mL) Sweet Potatoes and Cottage Cheese (page 153) • Breast or formula feeding	• ½ cup (125 mL) Over-the-Top Applesauce (page 140) • Whole wheat toast with margarine • Breast or formula feeding
Snack	• ¼ cup (50 mL) puffed rice cereal, dry • Diced fresh peaches • Water	• Animal-shaped cookie • Sliced grapes • Water	• ¼ cup (125 mL) Mango, Banana and Cottage Cheese (page 152) • Water
Supper	• ½ cup (125 mL) Turkey with Cranberries (page 123) • ¼ cup (50 mL) Mango (page 32) • Breast or formula feeding	• ½ cup (125 mL) Cheesy Broccoli and Ham Pasta (page 160) • Diced ripe pears • Breast or formula feeding	• ½ cup (125 mL) Shepherd's Pie (page 128) • ¼ cup (125 mL) Apples (page 26) • Breast or formula feeding
Snack	• Breast or formula feeding	• Breast or formula feeding	• Breast or formula feeding

Lemon Raspberry Yogurt

½ cup	fresh or frozen raspberries	125 mL
1 ½ cups	vanilla-flavored yogurt	375 mL
	Grated zest and juice of 1 lemon	

1. Place raspberries, yogurt, lemon zest and lemon juice in blender and purée on high speed until smooth and well combined.

2. *Make ahead:* Store in an airtight container in the refrigerator for up to 1 week.

**Nutritional Information
(Per ¼-cup/60 mL Serving)**

Calories	34 Kcal
Total Carbohydrates	4 g
Fiber	1 g
Fat	2 g
Protein	2 g
Iron	0 mg

**MAKES ABOUT
2 CUPS (500 ML)**

Adding your own fruit purée to plain yogurt is a much healthier option than using store-bought varieties.

TIPS

The bacteria found in plain yogurt, called lactobacillus, works to maintain a balance in the intestinal tract. It is easy for little systems to digest. Avoid yogurts with preservatives, additives and coloring.

Avoid low-fat and no-fat dairy products for at least the first two years of your child's life. A child's brain needs fat for full development.

VARIATION

Use an equal amount of any fruit you have on hand for a different flavor every day.

Over-the-Top Applesauce

Fat is an essential nutrient for your little one's brain development. Adding creamy ricotta to a favorite fruit or vegetable is a great way to pack in calories when they're going through a growth spurt and aren't eating as much as you'd like.

FOR OLDER KIDS

Serve over pound cake.

4 cups	sliced peeled Golden Delicious apples (about 5)	1 L
½ cup	unsweetened apple juice	125 mL
¼ cup	ricotta or mascarpone cheese	50 mL
1 tsp	ground cinnamon	5 mL
½ tsp	grated lemon zest	2 mL
¼ tsp	ground ginger	1 mL
¼ tsp	ground nutmeg	1 mL

1. In a medium saucepan, combine apples with apple juice. Cover and simmer until apples break down and are very tender.

2. Transfer to blender and add ricotta, cinnamon, lemon zest, ginger and nutmeg; purée on high speed until smooth.

3. *Make ahead:* Store in an airtight container in the refrigerator for up to 1 week.

**Nutritional Information
(Per ¼-cup/50 mL Serving)**

Calories	46 Kcal
Total Carbohydrates	8 g
Fiber	1 g
Fat	1 g
Protein	1 g
Iron	0 mg

Banana Cherry Blast

1	very ripe banana	1
½ cup	pitted sour cherries	125 mL
¼ cup	cherry juice (drained from cherries)	50 mL
½ cup	plain yogurt	125 mL

1. Place banana, cherries, cherry juice and yogurt in blender and purée on high speed until smooth.

2. *Make ahead:* Store in an airtight container in the refrigerator for up to 3 days. Do not freeze.

**Nutritional Information
(Per ½-cup/125 mL Serving)**

Calories	149 Kcal
Total Carbohydrates	31 g
Fiber	2 g
Fat	2 g
Protein	3 g
Iron	0 mg

**MAKES ABOUT
1 CUP (250 ML)**

Cherries make everyday bananas out of this world!

TIP

Substitute jarred sour cherries when you can't find fresh or frozen.

FOR OLDER KIDS

This makes a great smoothie for older children — and adults too!

9

MAKES 4 SERVINGS

A simple creamy dessert just for baby!

TIP

Replace the banana and raspberries with ½ cup (125 mL) of any of your little one's favorite fruit purées from previous chapters.

Fruit Custard

Preheat oven to 350°F (180°C)
Four 6-oz (175 mL) ramekins
Large baking pan

2	egg yolks	2
½ cup	homogenized (whole) milk	125 mL
¼ cup	sliced banana	50 mL
¼ cup	raspberries	50 mL
½ tsp	grated lemon zest	2 mL

1. Place egg yolks, milk, banana, raspberries and zest in blender; purée on high speed until very smooth.

2. Pour into ramekins and arrange in baking pan. Pour in boiling water to reach halfway up the sides of the ramekins. Bake in preheated oven until custard is set, about 30 minutes. Serve warm or chilled.

3. *Make ahead:* Store in an airtight container in the refrigerator for up to 3 days.

Nutritional Information (Per Serving)	
Calories	66 Kcal
Total Carbohydrates	6 g
Fiber	1 g
Fat	4 g
Protein	3 g
Iron	Trace

Polenta with Apricots

½ cup	dried apricots, chopped	125 mL
1 ½ cups	low-sodium chicken stock	375 mL
½ cup	cornmeal	125 mL
¼ cup	plain yogurt	50 mL

1. In a medium saucepan, bring apricots and chicken stock to a boil. Gradually stir in cornmeal until well combined. Reduce heat and simmer, stirring frequently, until mixture is creamy. Let cool slightly.

2. Transfer to blender, add yogurt and purée on high speed until smooth.

**MAKES ABOUT
2 CUPS (500 ML)**

Mild, creamy polenta blends beautifully with apricots and yogurt.

**Nutritional Information
(Per ¼-cup/50 mL Serving)**

Calories	80 Kcal
Total Carbohydrates	12 g
Fiber	1 g
Fat	2 g
Protein	3 g
Iron	0 mg

9

**MAKES ABOUT
2 CUPS (500 ML)**

FOR OLDER KIDS

This makes a great
sandwich spread, with
extra slices of banana
in between slices of
whole wheat bread.

Avocado, Banana and Yogurt

1	banana	1
1	avocado, peeled and pitted	1
½ cup	plain yogurt	125 mL

1. Place banana, avocado and yogurt in blender and
purée on high speed until smooth.

2. *Make ahead:* Store in an airtight container in the
refrigerator for up to 3 days. Do not freeze.

**Nutritional Information
(Per ¼-cup/50 mL Serving)**

Calories. . . . . 65 Kcal
Total Carbohydrates . . . . 9 g
Fiber . . . . 1 g
Fat . . . . 3 g
Protein . . . . 1 g
Iron . . . . 0 mg

Creamy Sweet Corn

1 tbsp	butter	15 mL
2 cups	frozen corn kernels, thawed	500 mL
½ cup	water	125 mL
¼ cup	sour cream	50 mL

MAKES ABOUT 2 CUPS (500 ML)

1. In a skillet, melt butter over medium-high heat. Add corn and stir to coat. Add water. Cover, reduce heat to medium and cook until corn is very soft, about 10 minutes. Let cool.

2. Transfer to blender, add sour cream and purée on high speed until smooth.

TIPS

Substitute an equal amount of plain yogurt for the sour cream.

For a little zip, add ¼ tsp (1 mL) grated orange zest.

**Nutritional Information
(Per ¼-cup/50 mL Serving)**

Calories	64 Kcal
Total Carbohydrates	9 g
Fiber	1 g
Fat	3 g
Protein	1 g
Iron	Trace

Using short or medium grain rice gives a creamy texture without extra fat in this nutritious classic treat.

Creamy Brown Rice Pudding

¼ cup	short-grain brown rice, rinsed	50 mL
¼ cup	water	50 mL
1 ½ cups	homogenized (whole) milk	375 mL
¼ cup	packed brown sugar	50 mL
1 tbsp	vanilla	15 mL
¼ cup	currants (optional)	50 mL

1. In a small saucepan, combine brown rice and water; bring to a boil over medium-high heat. Cover, reduce heat to low and simmer until most of liquid has been absorbed, about 20 minutes. Stir in milk, brown sugar, vanilla and currants (if using); increase heat to medium-high and bring to a boil, stirring often. Reduce heat to medium and simmer, stirring often, until rice is a porridge consistency, about 30 minutes. Let cool slightly.

2. Transfer to blender and purée on high speed to desired consistency.

**Nutritional Information
(Per ¼-cup/50 mL Serving)**

Calories. . . . . 71 Kcal
Total Carbohydrates. . . . . 12 g
Fiber . . . . 0 g
Fat . . . . 2 g
Protein . . . . 2 g
Iron . . . . Trace

Fruity Breakfast Rice

½ cup	medium-grain brown rice, rinsed	125 mL
½ cup	homogenized (whole) milk (approx.)	125 mL
½ cup	water	125 mL
1 tsp	vanilla	5 mL
½ tsp	ground cinnamon	2 mL
½ tsp	salt	2 mL
¼ cup	sliced banana	50 mL
¼ cup	chopped strawberries	50 mL

1. In a medium saucepan, combine rice, milk, water, vanilla, cinnamon and salt. Bring to a boil over medium-high heat. Cover, reduce heat to low and simmer, stirring occasionally, until liquid has been absorbed, about 50 minutes. Let cool.

2. Transfer to blender and add bananas and strawberries; purée on high speed until smooth. Serve warm with additional milk, if desired, for added creaminess.

MAKES ABOUT 2 CUPS (500 ML)

The rice is a nice change from oatmeal.

TIP

Sprinkle with a teaspoon of wheat germ for an extra fiber boost!

VARIATION

Replace bananas and strawberries with any fruit your child enjoys.

Nutritional Information (Per ¼-cup/50 mL Serving)

Calories	108 Kcal
Total Carbohydrates	17 g
Fiber	4 g
Fat	2 g
Protein	6 g
Iron	2 mg

*Barley is an excellent
source of water-soluble
fiber and is said to
have anti-diarrheal
properties.*

TIP

Choose pearl barley
— it doesn't need to be
presoaked and cooks in
half the time it takes
pot barley.

Barley with Apples and Dates

2	dates, pitted and chopped	2
1 cup	chopped peeled apples	250 mL
1 cup	homogenized (whole) milk	250 mL
1/2 cup	barley	125 mL

1. In a medium saucepan, over medium-high heat, bring dates, apples, milk and barley just to a boil. Cover, reduce heat to low and simmer until barley is tender, about 45 minutes. Let cool.

2. Transfer to blender and purée on high speed until smooth.

**Nutritional Information
(Per 1/4-cup/50 mL Serving)**

Calories. . . . . .74 Kcal
Total Carbohydrates . . . . .14 g
Fiber . . . . .2 g
Fat . . . . .1 g
Protein . . . . .3 g
Iron . . . . .Trace

Cauliflower, Spinach and Sweet Potato Curry

1 tbsp	vegetable oil	15 mL
¼ cup	chopped onion	50 mL
1 tsp	black mustard seeds	5 mL
2 tsp	mild curry paste	10 mL
1 cup	homogenized (whole) milk	250 mL
½ cup	vegetable or low-sodium chicken stock	125 mL
1 cup	chopped cauliflower	250 mL
½ cup	chopped peeled sweet potato	125 mL
1 cup	chopped fresh spinach	250 mL

1. In a skillet, heat oil over medium-high heat. Add onion and cook, stirring, until tender, about 5 minutes. Add mustard seeds and curry paste; cook, stirring, for 1 minute. Stir in milk and chicken stock; bring just to a boil. Add cauliflower and sweet potato. Cover, reduce heat to low and simmer until vegetables are very tender, about 15 minutes. Stir in spinach, remove from heat and let cool.

2. Transfer to blender and purée on high speed to desired consistency.

Nutritional Information (Per ¼-cup/50 mL Serving)	
Calories	58 Kcal
Total Carbohydrates	5 g
Fiber	1 g
Fat	3 g
Protein	2 g
Iron	Trace

MAKES ABOUT 2 CUPS (500 ML)

Don't be afraid to begin introducing new flavors. Mild curry paste adds flavor without heat in this nutritious meal.

TIP

Serve over cooked basmati rice for the whole family.

Use up leftover vegetable purée with this simple main dish that can be cut into portable pieces.

Vegetable Frittata

Preheat oven to 325°F (160°C)
8-inch (2 L) square glass baking dish, brushed with vegetable oil

4	egg yolks	4
¼ cup	vegetable purée (any flavor), thawed	50 mL
¼ cup	homogenized (whole) milk	50 mL
¼ cup	shredded Cheddar cheese	50 mL

1. Place egg yolks, vegetable purée and milk in blender; purée on high speed until well combined and smooth.

2. Pour egg mixture into prepared baking dish and sprinkle with cheese. Bake in preheated oven until eggs are puffed and set, about 35 minutes. Let cool slightly. Cut into bite-size pieces and serve.

Nutritional Information (Per Serving)	
Calories	117 Kcal
Total Carbohydrates	2 g
Fiber	0 g
Fat	10 g
Protein	6 g
Iron	1 mg

Fruity Cottage Cheese

½ cup	drained and rinsed canned mandarin orange segments	125 mL
½ cup	sliced strawberries	125 mL
½ cup	sliced peach	125 mL
½ cup	2% cottage cheese	125 mL
¼ cup	unsweetened peach nectar	50 mL

1. Place oranges, strawberries, peach, cottage cheese and peach nectar in blender and purée on high speed until blended.

2. *Make ahead:* Store in an airtight container in the refrigerator for up to 3 days. Do not freeze.

Nutritional Information
(Per ¼-cup/50 mL Serving)

Calories	30 Kcal
Total Carbohydrates	5 g
Fiber	1 g
Fat	0 g
Protein	2 g
Iron	0 mg

MAKES ABOUT 2 CUPS (500 ML)

Adding cottage cheese to fruit or vegetables is a quick way to get in some protein on action-packed days (aren't they all?).

TIP

Use thawed frozen fruit mixes when fresh fruits aren't available.

**MAKES ABOUT
2 CUPS (500 ML)**

FOR OLDER KIDS

Serve as a dip with celery sticks and pieces of apple and pear.

Mango, Banana and Cottage Cheese

1	banana	1
1	mango, peeled, pitted and cubed	1
½ cup	small-curd cottage cheese	125 mL

1. Place banana, mango and cottage cheese in blender and purée on high speed until smooth.

2. *Make ahead:* Store in an airtight container in the refrigerator for up to 3 days. Do not freeze.

**Nutritional Information
(Per ¼-cup/50 mL Serving)**

Calories	43 Kcal
Total Carbohydrates	8 g
Fiber	1 g
Fat	0 g
Protein	2 g
Iron	0 mg

Sweet Potatoes and Cottage Cheese

2 cups	cubed peeled sweet potatoes (about 2 small)	500 mL
½ cup	unsweetened apple juice	125 mL
½ cup	small-curd cottage cheese	125 mL

1. Arrange sweet potatoes in a steamer basket fitted over a medium saucepan of boiling water. Cover and steam until potatoes are very tender, about 20 minutes. Let cool.

2. Transfer to blender and add apple juice and cottage cheese; purée on high speed until well combined.

Nutritional Information (Per ¼-cup/50 mL Serving)	
Calories	46 Kcal
Total Carbohydrates	8 g
Fiber	1 g
Fat	0 g
Protein	2 g
Iron	0 mg

MAKES ABOUT 2 CUPS (500 ML)

Adding cottage cheese to vegetables makes for a protein-rich meal.

**MAKES ABOUT
2 CUPS (500 ML)**

*Creamy ricotta balances
the acidity of spinach
and tomatoes.*

TIPS

Fresh spinach is very
sandy and must be
washed thoroughly in
a large basin of water.
Change the water if
necessary. Trim woody
stems for even cooking.

Steaming spinach
tends to bring out its
bitterness. Instead,
cook it in a covered
saucepan, over high
heat, in the liquid that
remains on the leaves
after washing.

FOR OLDER KIDS

Stir into cooked pasta.

Spinach and Tomatoes with Ricotta

1 tbsp	olive oil	15 mL
1	clove garlic, minced	1
½ cup	canned diced tomatoes, with juice	125 mL
2 cups	trimmed spinach	500 mL
¼ cup	ricotta cheese	50 mL
2 tsp	freshly squeezed lemon juice	10 mL

1. In a skillet, heat oil over medium heat. Add garlic
and tomatoes with juice; cook until garlic is fragrant
but not browned, about 2 minutes. Stir in spinach
and cook until completely wilted, about 3 minutes.
Let cool.

2. Transfer to blender and add ricotta and lemon
juice; purée on high speed until smooth.

Nutritional Information (Per ¼-cup/50 mL Serving)	
Calories	35 Kcal
Total Carbohydrates	3 g
Fiber	0 g
Fat	3 g
Protein	1 g
Iron	0 mg

Spinach Surprise

1 tbsp	olive oil	15 mL
¼ cup	minced onion	50 mL
1	package (10 oz/300 g) fresh spinach, tough stems removed	1
½ cup	half-and-half (10 %) cream	125 mL
¼ cup	grated Parmesan cheese	50 mL

1. In a skillet, heat oil over medium-high heat. Add onion and cook, stirring, until tender, about 5 minutes. Add spinach and cream. Cover and cook until spinach has wilted, about 3 minutes. Remove from heat and let cool slightly.

2. Transfer to blender, add Parmesan and purée on high speed until just combined.

Nutritional Information
(Per ¼-cup/50 mL Serving)

Calories. . . . . 56 Kcal
Total Carbohydrates . . . . 2 g
Fiber . . . . 1 g
Fat . . . . 4 g
Protein . . . . 3 g
Iron . . . . 1 mg

**MAKES ABOUT
2 CUPS (500 ML)**

Surprise! The cheese eliminates any bitterness from the spinach.

Cauliflower is the most easily digestible member of the cabbage family and is an excellent source of vitamin C and potassium.

Tomato, Cauliflower and Cheese

2 tsp	olive oil	10 mL
¼ cup	chopped onion	50 mL
1 cup	cauliflower florets	250 mL
½ cup	canned diced tomatoes, with juice	125 mL
¼ cup	shredded Cheddar cheese	50 mL

1. In a skillet, heat oil over medium-high heat. Add onion and cook, stirring occasionally, until tender, but not browned, about 5 minutes. Add cauliflower and tomatoes with juice. Cover, reduce heat and simmer until cauliflower is tender, about 10 minutes. Let cool.

2. Transfer to blender, add cheese and purée on high speed until smooth.

**Nutritional Information
(Per ¼-cup/50 mL Serving)**

Calories.................................32 Kcal
Total Carbohydrates.........................2 g
Fiber ....1 g
Fat ....2 g
Protein ....1 g
Iron ....0 mg

Broccoli and Cauliflower Gratin

1 cup	broccoli florets	250 mL
1 cup	cauliflower florets	250 mL
1 cup	low-sodium vegetable stock	250 mL
1/2 cup	shredded Cheddar cheese	125 mL

1. In a medium saucepan, combine broccoli, cauliflower and vegetable stock; bring to a boil. Cover, reduce heat and simmer until vegetables are very tender, about 15 minutes. Let cool.

2. Transfer to blender, add cheese and purée on high speed until smooth.

Nutritional Information
(Per 1/4-cup/50 mL Serving)

Calories	40 Kcal
Total Carbohydrates	1 g
Fiber	1 g
Fat	2 g
Protein	4 g
Iron	0 mg

MAKES ABOUT 2 CUPS (500 ML)

Cauliflower mellows out the flavor of broccoli without compromising nutrients or taste.

TIP

To increase the fiber content of vegetable dishes, sprinkle with 1 tbsp (15 mL) wheat germ before puréeing. To maintain its freshness, store wheat germ in an airtight container in the refrigerator for up to 6 months or in the freezer for up to 1 year.

**MAKES ABOUT
2 CUPS (500 ML)**

*Serve fish as often as
you can to get your
little one on the road
to healthy eating.*

VARIATION

Substitute salmon for
the trout.

Fisherman's Pie

1	small Yukon gold potato, peeled and cubed	1
¼ cup	chopped onion	50 mL
4 oz	trout fillet (skin removed)	125 g
½ cup	frozen corn	125 mL
½ cup	broccoli florets	125 mL
¼ cup	shredded Cheddar cheese	50 mL

1. Place potato in a small saucepan of salted water. Bring to a boil over medium-high heat and cook until potato is tender, about 15 minutes. Drain.

2. Meanwhile, in a skillet, heat oil over medium-high heat. Add onion and cook until tender, about 5 minutes. Add trout, browning on both sides. Stir in corn and broccoli; cover and cook until fish flakes easily when pierced with a fork and broccoli is tender, about 5 minutes. Let cool.

3. Transfer to blender and add potatoes and cheese; purée on high speed to desired consistency.

**Nutritional Information
(Per ½-cup/125 mL Serving)**

Calories	63 Kcal
Total Carbohydrates	12 g
Fiber	1 g
Fat	0 g
Protein	4 g
Iron	1 mg

Cheesy Beef Casserole

6 oz	lean ground sirloin beef	175 g
¼ cup	chopped onion	50 mL
½ cup	chopped peeled carrot	125 mL
1 cup	canned diced tomatoes, with juice	250 mL
½ cup	shredded Cheddar cheese	125 mL
	Water (optional)	

1. In a skillet, brown beef over medium-high heat, breaking up any large pieces, until no longer pink, about 5 minutes. Drain off fat and return beef to skillet. Add onion, carrot and tomatoes with juice. Cover and cook, stirring occasionally, until onion and carrot are tender, about 10 minutes. Let cool.

2. Transfer to blender, add cheese and purée on high speed to desired consistency, adding water if necessary.

Nutritional Information
(Per ½-cup/125 mL Serving)

Calories	200 Kcal
Total Carbohydrates	7 g
Fiber	1 g
Fat	13 g
Protein	15 g
Iron	2 mg

MAKES ABOUT 2 CUPS (500 ML)

This quick skillet supper is good for every age!

FOR OLDER KIDS

Stir ½ cup (125 mL) purée into 1 cup (250 mL) cooked elbow noodles or any favorite pasta. This recipe is much more nutritious than packaged varieties.

*Kids can't get enough
pasta, so get in the
habit of making simple
pasta dishes and avoid
packaged varieties.*

Cheesy Broccoli and Ham Pasta

½ cup	pastini	125 mL
1 cup	broccoli florets	250 mL
½ cup	diced cooked ham (about 4 oz/125 g)	125 mL
½ cup	herb-flavored cream cheese	125 mL

1. Add pastini and broccoli to a saucepan of boiling water; cook until tender, about 10 minutes. Drain, reserving ¼ cup (50 mL) of the cooking liquid. Stir in ham, cream cheese and reserved cooking liquid until well combined.

2. Transfer to blender and purée on high speed to desired consistency.

**Nutritional Information
(Per ½-cup/125 mL Serving)**

Calories	206 Kcal
Total Carbohydrates	12 g
Fiber	1 g
Fat	13 g
Protein	9 g
Iron	1 mg
Vitamin C	24 mg

FOOD FOR BABIES

Twelve Months and Older

Meal Plans

At this age, formula-fed babies can be switched to homogenized (whole) milk. Breastfed babies can continue breastfeeding into their second year or can be switched to whole milk.

Toddlers eat erratically. You may have more success if you feed when your child is hungry rather than at particular times. Remember to include all the food groups: grain products, vegetables and fruits, milk products and meat and alternatives. Each food group provides unique nutrients, so it is important to offer your child a variety of foods from each food group every day. A good rule of thumb is to aim for three of the four food groups at each meal and one or two of the food groups at each snack. This will ensure that your child gets all the nutrients he or she needs to grow and develop.

See the introduction for more information on these meal plans.

MEAL	1	2	3
Breakfast	• 2 Multigrain Pancakes (page 168) spread with Figgy Pears (page 60) • ½ cup (125 mL) homogenized (whole) milk	• 1 Nutty Waffle (page 167) • ¼ cup (50 mL) Apricots, Pears and Tofu (page 135) • ½ cup (125 mL) homogenized (whole) milk	• Breakfast Toast Strips (page 171) with Fruity Yogurt Dip (page 174) • ¼ cup (50 mL) Rhubarb, Apples and Berries (page 64) • ½ cup (125 mL) homogenized (whole) milk
Snack	• ¼ cup (50 mL) Melon Madness (page 62) • Animal-shaped cookies • ½ cup (125 mL) apple juice, diluted with water	• Mini muffin • ½ cup (125 mL) apple juice, diluted with water	• ¼ cup (125 mL) Avocado, Banana and Yogurt (page 144) • ½ cup (125 mL) apple juice, diluted with water
Lunch	• Cheese sandwich on whole wheat bread • ¼ cup (125 mL) Orange Banana Smoothie (page 164) • ½ cup (125 mL) homogenized (whole) milk	• ¼ cup (125 mL) Guacamole for Beginners (page 82) • Pita wedges • Cubed cheese • ½ cup (125 mL) homogenized (whole) milk	• ¼ cup (125 mL) Polenta with Apricots (page 143) • Sliced grapes • ½ cup (125 mL) homogenized (whole) milk
Snack	• ¼ cup (125 mL) Fruity Cottage Cheese (page 151) • Whole wheat crackers • Water	• ¼ cup (125 mL) Over-the-Top Applesauce (page 140) • Animal-shaped cookies • Water	• ¼ cup (125 mL) toasted oat cereal, dry • Fruity Frosty Shake (page 165) • Water
Supper	• ½ cup (125 mL) Chicken with Brown Rice and Peas (page 117) • Cooked carrot coins • ¼ cup (125 mL) Blueberry Apricot Crumble (page 172) • ½ cup (125 mL) homogenized (whole) milk	• ½ cup (125 mL) Chicken Jambalaya (page 122) • Cooked chopped broccoli • ½ cup (125 mL) homogenized (whole) milk	• ¼ cup (50 mL) cooked cubed chicken • ½ cup (125 mL) Broccoli and Cauliflower Melt (page 178) • Sliced ripe pears • ½ cup (125 mL) homogenized (whole) milk
Snack	• ½ banana • ½ cup (125 mL) homogenized (whole) milk	• ¼ cup (125 mL) toasted oat cereal, dry • ½ cup (125 mL) homogenized (whole) milk	• Animal-shaped cookies • ½ cup (125 mL) homogenized (whole) milk

Smoothies are an excellent way to pack extra vitamins and nutrients into your child's day.

TIP

Use whole oranges in place of juice whenever possible. Make sure to remove peel, pith and seeds, which are bitter.

Orange Banana Smoothie

| 1 | banana | 1 |
| 1 cup | sliced peeled orange (about 1) | 250 mL |

1. In blender, combine banana and orange and purée on high speed until smooth.

**Nutritional Information
(Per ¼-cup/50 mL Serving)**

Calories	101 Kcal
Total Carbohydrates	26 g
Fiber	3 g
Fat	0 g
Protein	1 g
Iron	0 mg

MAKES 2 SERVINGS

This is a family favorite and great for a nutritious snack in a hurry!

VARIATION

Substitute chocolate cow's milk for the soy milk.

Nutty Choco' Monkey

1	banana	1
1 cup	chocolate-flavored soy milk	250 mL
½ cup	crushed ice	125 mL
¼ cup	smooth peanut butter	50 mL

1. In blender, on high speed, purée banana, soy milk, ice and peanut butter until smooth.

Nutritional Information (Per Serving)

Calories	350 Kcal
Total Carbohydrates	33 g
Fiber	3 g
Fat	21 g
Protein	3 g
Iron	1 mg

Fruity Frosty Shake

1 cup	homogenized (whole) milk	250 mL
½ cup	crushed ice	125 mL
½ cup	chopped peeled pear	125 mL
¼ cup	frozen berries	50 mL

1. In blender, on high speed, purée milk, ice, pear and berries until smooth and slushy.

Nutritional Information (Per Serving)

Calories	111 Kcal
Total Carbohydrates	15 g
Fiber	2 g
Fat	4 g
Protein	4 g
Iron	0 mg

MAKES 2 SERVINGS

For a simple, nutritious treat, blend ripe seasonal fruit with ice and milk.

VARIATIONS

Substitute soy or rice milk for the milk.

Substitute 1 cup (250 mL) frozen fruit purée for the pear and berries and omit the ice.

Simple Fruit Sorbet

½ cup	frozen peach purée	125 mL
½ cup	unsweetened apple juice	125 mL

1. In blender, on high speed, purée peach purée and juice until smooth. Serve immediately.

Nutritional Information (Per ½ Serving)

Calories	131 Kcal
Total Carbohydrates	33 g
Fiber	3 g
Fat	0 g
Protein	1 g
Iron	1 mg

MAKES 1 SERVING

Is your freezer still full of containers of delicious fruit purées! Now that your little one is getting older, here is a quick treat idea.

VARIATION

Substitute any fruit purée for the peach purée and any flavor juice for the apple juice.

**MAKES ABOUT
1 CUP (250 ML)**

This recipe can be mixed with formula or with any fruit or vegetable purée to increase fiber intake. Try it in Blueberry Apricot Crumble (page 172) or Blue Nectarine Yogurt (page 173).

TIP

This recipe is suitable for babies nine months and older if the almonds are omitted.

Mixed Grains

**Preheat oven to 350°F (180°C)
Rimmed baking sheet**

1 cup	old-fashioned rolled oats	250 mL
¼ cup	bran cereal	50 mL
¼ cup	unblanched almonds (optional)	50 mL
2 tbsp	wheat germ	25 mL

1. Spread oats, bran cereal, almonds (if using) and wheat germ on baking sheet. Bake in preheated oven until fragrant and lightly toasted, about 7 minutes. Let cool.

2. Transfer toasted grains to blender and purée on high speed until smooth.

3. *Make ahead:* Store in an airtight container in a cool place for up to 1 month.

**Nutritional Information
(Per ¼-cup/50 mL Serving)**

Calories	158 Kcal
Total Carbohydrates	22 g
Fiber	6 g
Fat	6 g
Protein	6 g
Iron	2 mg

Nutty Waffles

MAKES 12 WAFFLES

If you don't have a waffle iron, this batter will work for pancakes too. Top with slices of banana and berries for a treat.

Preheated waffle iron, greased

3	eggs	3
1 ½ cups	homogenized (whole) milk	375 mL
¼ cup	butter, melted	50 mL
1 ½ cups	all-purpose flour	375 mL
½ cup	ground toasted pecans or walnuts	125 mL
1 tbsp	baking powder	15 mL
1 tbsp	granulated sugar	15 mL
½ tsp	salt	2 mL

1. In blender, on high speed, purée eggs, milk and butter until smooth. Sprinkle with flour, pecans, baking powder, sugar and salt. Pulse on low speed just until combined (mixture will be lumpy). Do not overmix or waffles will be tough.

2. Spoon ½ cup (125 mL) batter into hot waffle iron, spreading with spatula. Close lid and cook for 5 to 7 minutes, until golden-brown and no longer steaming. Remove to a plate and keep warm. Repeat with remaining batter.

3. *Make ahead:* Store waffles in an airtight container, layered between waxed paper or parchment paper, in the refrigerator for up to 1 day or in the freezer for up to 3 months. To serve, toast frozen waffles in toaster until warmed through.

TIP

Toast nuts in a dry skillet over medium-high heat until fragrant, about 3 minutes, to intensify their flavor. Watch carefully — if they scorch, they will be bitter.

Nutritional Information (Per Waffle)	
Calories	160 Kcal
Total Carbohydrates	16 g
Fiber	1 g
Fat	9 g
Protein	4 g
Iron	1 mg

*Mix up the dry
ingredients ahead
of time, and your
very own nutritious
pancake mix will be
ready when you are!
Store in an airtight
container for up to
1 month.*

TIP

Add extra nutrients to
maple syrup by mixing
1/4 cup (50 mL) of
your child's favorite
fruit purée with 1/4 cup
(50 mL) maple syrup.

Multigrain Pancakes

3	eggs	3
1 1/2 cups	homogenized (whole) milk	375 mL
1/4 cup	butter, melted	50 mL
1/4 cup	liquid honey	50 mL
1 cup	whole wheat flour	250 mL
1/2 cup	all-purpose flour	125 mL
1/2 cup	old-fashioned rolled oats	125 mL
1/4 cup	cornmeal	50 mL
1/4 cup	packed brown sugar	50 mL
2 tsp	baking powder	10 mL
1 tsp	salt	5 mL
1/2 tsp	baking soda	2 mL
1/2 tsp	ground cinnamon	2 mL
2 tsp	butter (approx.)	10 mL

1. In blender, on high speed, purée eggs, milk, melted
   butter and honey until smooth. Sprinkle in whole
   wheat and all-purpose flours, oats, cornmeal,
   brown sugar, baking powder, salt, baking soda and
   cinnamon. Pulse on low speed just until combined
   (mixture will be lumpy). Do not overmix or
   pancakes will be tough.

2. In a skillet, melt some of the 2 tsp (5 mL) butter over medium heat. Pour in $\frac{1}{4}$ cup (50 mL) batter for each pancake, leaving room for spreading. Cook until tops of pancakes are speckled with bubbles; turn and cook until undersides are golden, about 1 minute. Remove to a plate and keep warm. Repeat with remaining batter, adding more butter to the skillet as necessary.

3. *Make ahead:* Store pancakes in an airtight container, layered between waxed paper or parchment paper, in the refrigerator for up to 1 day or in the freezer for up to 3 months. To serve, toast frozen pancakes in toaster until warmed through.

Nutritional Information (Per Pancake)	
Calories	138 Kcal
Total Carbohydrates	20 g
Fiber	1 g
Fat	5 g
Protein	4 g
Iron	1 mg

*These make great
dippers for soup and
chili — or fill with jam
for a tasty sandwich.*

VARIATIONS

Add 1 cup (250 mL)
corn kernels to batter.

To make small,
handheld snacks,
use 1 tbsp (15 mL)
of the batter to make
each cake.

MAKE AHEAD

Store corncakes in an
airtight container,
layered between waxed
paper or parchment
paper, in the refrigerator
for up to 1 day or in
the freezer for up to
3 months. To serve,
place in a single layer
on a baking sheet
lined with parchment
paper in a 200°F
(100°C) oven until
warmed through,
about 15 minutes.

Buttermilk Corncakes

1	egg yolk	1
¾ cup	buttermilk	175 mL
1 tbsp	butter, melted	15 mL
½ cup	cornmeal	125 mL
¼ cup	all-purpose flour	50 mL
1 tsp	granulated sugar	5 mL
½ tsp	baking soda	2 mL
¼ tsp	salt	1 mL
2 tsp	vegetable oil (approx.)	10 mL

1. In blender, on high speed, purée egg yolk, buttermilk and butter until smooth. Sprinkle in cornmeal, flour, sugar, baking soda and salt. Pulse on low speed just until combined (mixture will be slightly lumpy).

2. In a skillet, heat 1 tsp (5 mL) of the oil over medium heat. Pour in ¼ cup (50 mL) batter for each corncake, leaving room for spreading. Cook, turning once, until both sides are golden, about 3 minutes per side. Remove to a plate and keep warm. Repeat with remaining batter, adding oil to the skillet as necessary.

Nutritional Information (Per Corncake)

Calories. . . . . 44 Kcal
Total Carbohydrates. . . . . 6 g
Fiber . . . . 0 g
Fat . . . . 2 g
Protein . . . . 1 g
Iron . . . . trace

Breakfast Toast Strips

1	egg	1
2 tbsp	homogenized (whole) milk	25 mL
½ tsp	vanilla	2 mL
½ tsp	grated orange zest	2 mL
¼ tsp	ground cinnamon	1 mL
2 tsp	butter	10 mL
1	slice whole wheat bread, cut into 1-inch (2.5 cm) strips	1
	Fruity Yogurt Dip (see recipe, page 174)	

MAKES 1 SERVING

These handheld strips are an excellent way to start the day. You can also pack them up for a snack on the go!

1. In blender, on high speed, purée egg, milk, vanilla, orange zest and cinnamon until smooth. Transfer to a shallow bowl or pie plate.

2. In a skillet, melt butter over medium heat. Dip bread strips in egg mixture, turning until well coated. Arrange in a single layer in skillet. Cook, turning once, until both sides are golden, about 3 minutes per side. Serve warm with Fruity Yogurt Dip.

Nutritional Information (Per Serving)

Calories	199 Kcal
Total Carbohydrates	17 g
Fiber	2 g
Fat	11 g
Protein	9 g
Iron	2 mg

**MAKES ABOUT
2 CUPS (500 ML)**

These two fruits are nutritional dynamos and provide a wonderful meal when combined with energy-boosting grains.

TIPS

When apricots are not in season, substitute dried apricots, which have a higher concentration of nutrients. Soak them in enough boiling water just to cover them for 30 minutes before using.

Top with a dollop of plain yogurt.

Blueberry Apricot Crumble

1 1/2 cups	sliced pitted apricots (4 to 5)	375 mL
1/2 cup	frozen wild blueberries, thawed	125 mL
1/4 cup	orange juice	50 mL
1/2 cup	Mixed Grains (see recipe, page 166)	125 mL

1. Place apricots, blueberries and orange juice in blender and purée on high speed until smooth.

2. Sprinkle with Mixed Grains. For softer grains, let sit for 5 minutes before serving.

**Nutritional Information
(Per 1/4-cup/50 mL Serving)**

Calories . . . . 59 Kcal
Total Carbohydrates . . . . 9 g
Fiber . . . . 2 g
Fat . . . . 2 g
Protein . . . . 2 g
Iron . . . . 0 mg

Blue Nectarine Yogurt

1 cup	sliced nectarines (about 2)	250 mL
¼ cup	fresh or thawed frozen blueberries	50 mL
1 cup	plain yogurt	250 mL
1 cup	Mixed Grains (see recipe, page 166)	250 mL

1. Place nectarines and blueberries in blender and purée on high speed until smooth.

2. Transfer to a medium bowl and stir in yogurt.

3. For each serving, mix ¼ cup (50 mL) yogurt mixture with 2 tbsp (25 mL) Mixed Grains. Let sit for 5 minutes before serving.

Nutritional Information
(Per ¼-cup/50 mL Serving)

Calories	136 Kcal
Total Carbohydrates	18 g
Fiber	4 g
Fat	5 g
Protein	5 g
Iron	0 mg

MAKES ABOUT 2 CUPS (500 ML)

Cereals based on oats provide long-lasting energy throughout the day. Mix them with your child's favorite fruit, yogurt or cottage cheese to get them through action-packed days.

TIP

Add milk to each serving as desired for a thinner consistency.

There will come a point when the only way to get your child to eat is to serve a dip alongside. Here are some quick, easy, nutritious options.

VARIATION

Substitute 1 cup (250 mL) of any fruit purée you have stored in your freezer for the options given here. Thaw before blending.

Fruity Yogurt and Cream Cheese Dips

Yogurt Base

½ cup	plain full-fat yogurt	125 mL
1 tbsp	liquid honey	15 mL

1. In blender, on low speed, blend yogurt and honey until smooth.

2. Blend with any of the fruit combinations that follow.

3. *Make ahead:* Store in an airtight container in the refrigerator for up to 3 days.

Nutritional Information (Per ½ Recipe)

Calories	70 Kcal	Fat	2 g
Total Carbohydrates	11 g	Protein	2 g
Fiber	0 g	Iron	0 mg

Cream Cheese Base

4 oz	spreadable cream cheese (½ package)	125 g
¼ cup	homogenized (whole) milk	50 mL

1. In blender, on low speed, blend cream cheese and milk until smooth.

2. Blend with any of the fruit combinations that follow.

3. *Make ahead:* Store in an airtight container in the refrigerator for up to 3 days.

Nutritional Information (Per ½ Recipe)

Calories	217 Kcal	Fat	21 g
Total Carbohydrates	3 g	Protein	5 g
Fiber	0 g	Iron	1 mg

Banana and Mango

| 1 | small banana, chopped | 1 |
| 1/2 cup | chopped peeled mango | 125 mL |

Nutritional Information (Per 1/2 Recipe)

Calories . . . . 81 Kcal   Fat . . . . 0 g
Total Carbohydrates. . 21 g   Protein . . . . 1 g
Fiber . . . . 2 g   Iron . . . . 0 mg

Apple and Apricot

1/2 cup	chopped peeled apple	125 mL
1/2 cup	chopped peeled apricots	125 mL
1/4 tsp	ground cinnamon	1 mL

Nutritional Information (Per 1/2 Recipe)

Calories . . . . 36 Kcal   Fat . . . . 0 g
Total Carbohydrates. . . 9 g   Protein . . . . 1 g
Fiber . . . . 2 g   Iron . . . . 0 mg

Peach and Orange

| 1/2 cup | chopped peeled peach | 125 mL |
| 1/2 cup | orange segments, white pith removed | 125 mL |

Nutritional Information (Per 1/2 Recipe)

Calories . . . . 39 Kcal   Fat . . . . 0 g
Total Carbohydrates. . 10 g   Protein . . . . 1 g
Fiber . . . . 2 g   Iron . . . . 0 mg

Continued on next page …

Tangerine and Kiwi

| ½ cup | tangerine segments | 125 mL |
| ½ cup | chopped peeled kiwi | 125 mL |

Nutritional Information (Per ½ Recipe)

Calories . . . . 48 Kcal   Fat . . . . 0 g
Total Carbohydrates . . 12 g   Protein . . . . 1 g
Fiber . . . . 3 g   Iron . . . . 0 mg

Strawberry and Lemon

1 cup	sliced strawberries	250 mL
1 tsp	grated lemon zest	5 mL
2 tsp	freshly squeezed lemon juice	10 mL

Nutritional Information (Per ½ Recipe)

Calories . . . . 27 Kcal   Fat . . . . 0 g
Total Carbohydrates . . . 6 g   Protein . . . . 1 g
Fiber . . . . 2 g   Iron . . . . 0 mg

Pear and Ginger

| 1 cup | chopped peeled pear | 250 mL |
| ½ tsp | ground ginger | 2 mL |

Nutritional Information (Per ½ Recipe)

Calories . . . . 51 Kcal   Fat . . . . 0 g
Total Carbohydrates . . 13 g   Protein . . . . 0 g
Fiber . . . . 2 g   Iron . . . . 0 mg

Very Berry Pears

3 cups	diced peeled pears (about 4)	750 mL
½ cup	water (approx.)	125 mL
¼ cup	raspberries	50 mL
¼ cup	blueberries	50 mL
1 tbsp	liquid honey (optional)	15 mL

1. In a medium saucepan, over medium-low heat, combine pears, water, raspberries, blueberries and honey (if using). Cover and simmer, stirring occasionally, until pears are very tender, about 30 minutes. Let cool.

2. Transfer to blender and purée on high speed, adding more water if necessary, until smooth.

Nutritional Information (Per ¼-cup/50 mL Serving)	
Calories	44 Kcal
Total Carbohydrates	11 g
Fiber	2 g
Fat	0 g
Protein	0 g
Iron	0 mg

MAKES ABOUT 2 CUPS (500 ML)

Raspberries and blueberries are packed with nutrients, but are too strong to offer to your baby on their own. Adding a few into pears is an economical, tasty solution.

TIP

This recipe is suitable for babies six months and older if the honey is omitted.

FOR OLDER KIDS

Turn ordinary porridge into something special by mixing in some of this purée, along with a sprinkle of toasted almonds.

Get in the habit of sprinkling wheat germ over all your veggies to sneak in some extra fiber.

TIP

Toasting nuts, seeds and grains brings out their flavor. Toast them on a rimmed baking sheet in a 350°F (180°C) oven until fragrant and lightly golden, about 5 minutes. Let cool before using.

Broccoli and Cauliflower Melt

1 cup	broccoli florets and peeled stems	250 mL
1 cup	cauliflower florets	250 mL
1 cup	homogenized (whole) milk	250 mL
2 tbsp	toasted old-fashioned rolled oats	25 mL
1 tbsp	wheat germ	15 mL
½ cup	shredded Cheddar cheese	125 mL

1. In a medium saucepan, over medium-high heat, combine broccoli, cauliflower, milk, oats and wheat germ; bring to a boil. Cover, reduce heat and simmer until vegetables are very tender, about 20 minutes. Stir in cheese. Let cool.

2. Transfer to blender and purée on high speed until smooth.

**Nutritional Information
(Per ¼-cup/50 mL Serving)**

Calories	61 Kcal
Total Carbohydrates	4 g
Fiber	1 g
Fat	4 g
Protein	4 g
Iron	0 mg

Ham with White Beans and Cabbage

2 tsp	olive oil	10 mL
½ cup	sliced onion	125 mL
½ cup	diced cooked ham (about 4 oz/125 g)	125 mL
2 cups	low-sodium chicken stock	500 mL
½ cup	dried white beans, soaked and drained (see tips, at left)	125 mL
1 cup	chopped green cabbage	250 mL

1. In a medium saucepan, heat oil over medium-high heat. Add onion and cook, stirring, until tender, about 5 minutes. Add ham and cook, stirring, until lightly browned, about 3 minutes. Stir in stock, scraping any brown bits from bottom of pan. Add beans; cover, reduce heat and simmer for 30 minutes. Stir in cabbage and simmer until beans and cabbage are tender, about 30 minutes. Let cool.

2. Transfer to blender and purée on high speed to desired consistency.

Nutritional Information
(Per ½-cup/125 mL Serving)

Calories	173 Kcal
Total Carbohydrates	20 g
Fiber	5 g
Fat	2 g
Protein	15 g
Iron	3 mg

MAKES ABOUT 2 CUPS (500 ML)

Most varieties of dried beans are excellent sources of potassium and folic acid, and they give a smooth, creamy consistency to purées.

TIPS

Soaking beans and legumes overnight decreases cooking time, preserves nutrients and reduces the flatulence they can cause.

Quick soak method: In a saucepan, combine 3 parts water with 1 part dried beans; bring to a boil over medium heat. Remove from heat and let stand, covered, for 1 to 2 hours. Drain. Cook according to recipe.

Add vegetable stock or more chicken stock to make a great soup for the whole family.

**MAKES 2 CUPS
(500 ML)**

*Sometimes we have to
be a bit sneaky when
our toddlers are going
through a "non-veggie"
stage... what they
don't know can be
good for them!*

TIP

Use this sauce in any
recipe that calls for
prepared pasta sauce.

Veggie Red Sauce

1 tbsp	olive oil	15 mL
1	clove garlic, minced	1
1 cup	chopped peeled carrots (about 2)	250 mL
½ cup	chopped peeled broccoli stems	125 mL
¼ cup	chopped onion	50 mL
1 cup	canned diced tomatoes, with juice	250 mL

1. In a skillet, heat oil over medium-high heat. Add garlic, carrots, broccoli stems and onion and stir to combine. Cook, stirring, until carrots are tender, about 7 minutes. Add tomatoes with juice, reduce heat and simmer until vegetables are very tender, about 15 minutes. Let cool.

2. Transfer to blender and purée on high speed until very smooth.

**Nutritional Information
(Per ¼-cup/50 mL Serving)**

Calories . . . . 33 Kcal
Total Carbohydrates . . . . 4 g
Fiber . . . . 1 g
Fat . . . . 2 g
Protein . . . . 1 g
Iron . . . . 0 mg

Veggie Cream Sauce

1 tbsp	olive oil	15 mL
1 cup	diced peeled carrots (about 2)	250 mL
½ cup	diced peeled broccoli stems	125 mL
¼ cup	diced onion	50 mL
1	clove garlic, minced	1
2 tbsp	cubed softened cream cheese	25 mL
1 cup	low-sodium chicken stock	250 mL

**MAKES ABOUT
2 CUPS (500 ML)**

Try this sauce over pastini or stirred into any meat purée to boost nutritional value and flavor.

1. In a skillet, heat oil over medium-high heat. Stir in carrots, broccoli, onion and garlic; cook, stirring often, until carrots are tender, about 5 minutes. Whisk in cream cheese and stock; bring just to a boil. Reduce heat and simmer, uncovered, until vegetables are very tender, about 10 minutes. Let cool.

2. Transfer to blender and purée on high speed until very smooth.

**Nutritional Information
(Per ¼-cup/50 mL Serving)**

Calories.	33 Kcal
Total Carbohydrates	4 g
Fiber	1 g
Fat	2 g
Protein	1 g
Iron	0 mg

Library and Archives Canada Cataloguing in Publication

Young, Nicole
    Blender baby food : over 125 recipes for healthy, homemade meals / Nicole Young.

ISBN 0-7788-0118-7

    1. Cookery (Baby foods) 2. Baby foods. 3. Blenders (Cookery)
4. Infants—Nutrition. I. Title.

TX740.O48 2005   641.5'6222   C2005-902566-2

Index

at Books
ert Rose

Baking

- 250 Best Cakes & Pies
  by Esther Brody
- 500 Best Cookies, Bars & Squares
  by Esther Brody
- 500 Best Muffin Recipes
  by Esther Brody
- 125 Best Cheesecake Recipes
  by George Geary
- 125 Best Chocolate Recipes
  by Julie Hasson
- 125 Best Chocolate Chip Recipes
  by Julie Hasson
- 125 Best Cupcake Recipes
  by Julie Hasson
- Complete Cake Mix Magic
  by Jill Snider

lthy Cooking

- 5 Best Vegetarian cipes
  Byron Ayanoglu h contributions from gis Kemezys
- nerica's Best okbook for ds with Diabetes
  Colleen Bartley
- anada's Best Cookbook for Kids with Diabetes
  by Colleen Bartley
- The Juicing Bible
  by Pat Crocker and Susan Eagles
- The Smoothies Bible
  by Pat Crocker

- 125 Best Vegan Recipes
  by Maxine Effenson Chuck and Beth Gurney
- 500 Best Healthy Recipes
  Edited by Lynn Roblin, RD
- 125 Best Gluten-Free Recipes
  by Donna Washburn and Heather Butt
- The Best Gluten-Free Family Cookbook
  by Donna Washburn and Heather Butt
- America's Everyday Diabetes Cookbook
  Edited by Katherine E. Younker, MBA, RD
- Canada's Everyday Diabetes Choice Recipes
  Edited by Katherine E. Younker, MBA, RD
- Canada's Complete Diabetes Cookbook
  Edited by Katherine E. Younker, MBA, RD
- The Best Diabetes Cookbook (U.S.)
  Edited by Katherine E. Younker, MBA, RD
- The Best Low-Carb Cookbook
  from Robert Rose

Recent Bestsellers

- 125 Best Soup Recipes
  by Marylin Crowley and Joan Mackie
- The Convenience Cook
  by Judith Finlayson
- 125 Best Ice Cream Recipes
  by Marilyn Linton and Tanya Linton

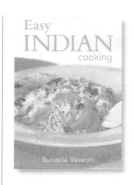

- Easy Indian Cooking
  by Suneeta Vaswani
- Simply Thai Cooking
  by Wandee Young and Byron Ayanoglu

Health

- The Complete Natural Medicine Guide to the 50 Most Common Medicinal Herbs
  by Dr. Heather Boon, B.Sc.Phm., Ph.D., and Michael Smith, B.Pharm, M.R.Pharm.S., ND
- The Complete Kid's Allergy and Asthma Guide
  Edited by Dr. Milton Gold
- The Complete Natural Medicine Guide to Breast Cancer
  by Sat Dharam Kaur, ND
- The Complete Doctor's Stress Solution
  by Penny Kendall-Reed, MSc, ND, and Dr. Stephen Reed, MD, FRCSC
- The Complete Doctor's Healthy Back Bible
  by Dr. Stephen Reed, MD, and Penny Kendall-Reed, MSc, ND, with Dr Michael Ford, MD, FRCSC, and Dr. Charles Gregory, MD, ChB, FRCP(C)
- Everyday Risks in Pregnancy & Breastfeeding
  by Dr. Gideon Koren, MD, FRCP(C), ND
- Help for Eating Disorders
  by Dr. Debra Katzman, MD, FRCP(C), and Dr. Leora Pinhas, MD

Also Available
from Robert Rose

BETTER FOOD FOR KIDS

Paperback ISBN 0-7788-0045-8
$24.95 Canada

Paperback ISBN 0-7788-0048-2
$17.95 U.S.

Hardcover ISBN 0 7788-0049-0
$27.95 U.S.

BETTER BABY FOOD

Paperback ISBN 0-7788-0030-X
$24.95 Canada

Paperback ISBN 0-7788-0027-X
$18.95 U.S.

Hardcover ISBN 0-7788-0032-6
$27.95 U.S.

For more great books, see previous pages